Acs

Doctor Johnson

DR. JOHNSON
From a Portrait by Sir Joshua Reynolds

DOCTOR
JOHNSON
A PLAY

By

A. EDWARD NEWTON, *Efq.*

Author of

The AMENITIES OF BOOK-COLLECTING *and* KINDRED AFFECTIONS	*A* MAGNIFICENT FARCE *& Other* DIVERSIONS *of a* BOOK-COLLECTOR

BOSTON
The ATLANTIC MONTHLY *Press*
MDCCCCXXIII

D. B. Updike, The Merrymount Press, Boston
Printed in the United States of America

To CECIL HARMSWORTH, *Esq.,*
M.P.

My dear Harmsworth:

In dedicating this Book to you, I do not doubt that I chiefly honour myfelf. You will, neverthelefs, accept it as a gefture of appreciation from "*The Plantations,*" as Dr. *Johnfon* called this Country.

You have made *1 7, Gough Square,* the houfe in which the *Dictionary* was written, a Shrine to which Johnfonians refort to do Honour to his Memory. And, Sir, in Johnfonian phrafe, you are to regard this flight Performance, if it be pleafing to you, as a Reward of Merit; and if otherwife, as "one of the Inconveniences of Eminence."

A. EDWARD NEWTON

By His *Majefty's* Company.

AT THE

Theatre Royal in *Drury-lane*,

This prefent *Seafon* being the SPRING of 1923,

The firft performance of

DR. JOHNSON

GIVEN BY AN IMMORTAL CAST INCLUDING

Sir JOSHUA REYNOLDS,

Mr. THRALE, Mr. BOSWELL,

Mr. GARRICK,

Mrs. THRALE, Mifs BURNEY,

Mr. BURKE, Mr. GOLDSMITH,

Mrs. WOFFINGTON, and Others

Adapted to the BOARDS (*with alterations*) by

MR. A. EDWARD NEWTON

A *Gentleman* of *Philadelphia* in *Pennfylvania.*

PLACES for the PERFORMANCE may now be fecured.
Nothing under FULL PRICE will be taken.

§§ *No Money to be taken at the Stage-door, nor any Money to be
returned after the Curtain is drawn up.*

‡‡ It is hop'd no Gentlemen will take it ill that they can't be admitted behind
the Scenes.

VIVANT REX & REGINA

A List of the
Illustrations.

Argument.

ANYONE *with a teaspoonful of imagination can read
this play with pleasure; with two teaspoonsful, I
will not be responsible for results. He, or she, may
be disappointed, for there is no plot to speak of. But there is
talk—about as good talk as has ever been reported, and
James* Boswell *as a reporter has never had an equal.*

*My own part in the work is very attenuated, as attenu-
ated as a piece of thread: it has to be, for on this slender
thread, of my own manufacture, I have elected to string
jewels, exquisite in cut and colour. It is believed that the
stones match and that the thread does not show—much.*

*The jewels are, most of them, genuine, a few are teclas;
and ardent* Johnsonians, *and* Boswellians *too, may amuse
themselves in sorting them out if they care to. I permit myself to remark that several experts have been deceived. For
several I am indebted to friends; for example, the letter on
page* 108 *was written many years ago, not by Dr.* Johnson,
but by an eminent Johnsonian *scholar, to Mrs.* Newton
*who greatly values it. Likewise the retort, "Madam, I take
refuge in incredulity," I got from Mrs.* John Markoe *who
had it from her father. The phrase is faultlessly* Johnsonian; *if it was originally* Johnson's, *I cannot put my
mental finger upon it. The reference to the Dictionary being
edited*

edited by a Scotch Presbyterian is an imitation of Johnson *which was doing double duty in the newspapers a few years ago. I do not know who set this ball a-rolling.*

. . . .

Amy Lowell, Caroline Sinkler, *and* Mrs. John Markoe *were invited to* Mrs. Thrale's *party but were unable to accept.* "*I don't care a fig for the defection of the females,*" Mrs. Thrale *remarked to her husband one morning over the breakfast table, tossing aside several notes;* "Elizabeth Carter *and* Hannah More *and* Mrs. Montagu *will be only too glad to take their places, but mark my words, it means that we shall lose the* Lord Primate, Edmund Burke *and* Charles Fox, *and I had rather counted on their adding lustre to the affair.*" "*Don't count your chickens before they are hatched, my dear,*" *said* Mr. Thrale. "*And,*" *he continued,* "*they will lose an excellent dinner.*"

. . . .

A word as to my cast. The greatest actor that England ever produced, as well as some of her greatest men; authors, artists, dramatists, and statesmen, grand ladies and women of the town, are included. It would be difficult to get such a company together nowadays. You may say that my actors are merely shadows: I stipulated that you were to have a teaspoonful of imagination; you remember that. For myself, at any rate, these people, all of them, are my very real friends. They are quite as real and much more interesting than most

of

of those among whom my lot is cast. Had I been in London *in the middle of the eighteenth century, should I have been privileged to know them as I know them now? I should say, or rather they would have said,* CERTAINLY NOT. *I am better off as I am, and perhaps you are too, Dear Reader.*

[*Exit* Author *carrying a short piece of thread which he had left over.*]

A. EDWARD NEWTON

"Oak Knoll," Daylesford
  Pennsylvania
    June 23, 1922

Topographical.

ACT I.

DR. JOHNSON'S HOUSE in Gough Square still exists; in his time it was a not unfashionable neighbourhood. It is believed to be the only one of Dr. Johnson's many London residences now remaining, and of all of them it is the most important, for in it Johnson lived for ten years, from 1748 to 1758, and in it he wrote the greater part of the Dictionary and several other of his more important literary works.

The house was acquired by Mr. Cecil Harmsworth, M.P., in 1911 and it remains his property, although it is understood that he may give it to the nation. After thoughtful and expensive alterations, which mercifully are but little in evidence, it has become one of the most visited of the small museums in London.

It is not exactly easy to find. After leaving the Griffin, the site of old Temple Bar, walking some distance east on the left hand side of Fleet Street and peering up (or down) a number of narrow courts with such seductive names as Johnson's Court (which, by the way, has no reference whatever to our Johnson) and Bolt Court, one comes upon Wine Office Court. Turning up (or down) one passes on the right, after a few steps, the Old Cheshire Cheese. The legend which associates this tavern with the great Lexicographer is a triumph of advertising, for there is no single contemporary reference connecting Johnson with it. It is, however, quite possible that he may have frequented it, as it was on his side of Fleet Street, which,

which, as an old man, he disliked to cross. Passing the Cheese a distance of perhaps fifty yards and turning sharply to the left, a short walk brings one into Gough Square, with the Johnson house on the opposite side.

And it is well worth a visit. It is now ninety years since Carlyle, "not without labour and risk," discovered it and wrote a description of it in his famous review of a new edition of Boswell's *Life of Johnson*. It is a substantial brick edifice of three stories and an attic. The front doorway deserves special attention, and the quaint chain bolt inside should not be overlooked. The stout old-fashioned oak balustraded stairs, which caught Carlyle's eye, still remain as evidence of the good workmanship of two hundred and odd years ago. The caretakers, who live in a tiny house near by, are excellent Johnsonians, and take pleasure in showing the house to the constantly increasing number of disciples of the dear old Doctor, in whom we know not what most to admire: his wisdom, his wit, or his character.

ACTS II & III.

THRALE PLACE, Mr. Henry Thrale's country residence at Streatham, was a large substantial mansion situated in an open and salubrious suburb about six miles out of London. The house itself has long since disappeared, and the once fine estate is now entirely built over, but the family name is preserved in the tiny almshouses established by Henry Thrale in the High Street, and in Thrale Street which runs through what was once the paddock.

ACT IV.

ACT IV.

Bolt Court is situated not many yards east of Gough Square. The house in which Dr. Johnson died was taken down many years ago to make room for a modern printing-house. A tablet let into the wall marks its location.

Act I.

Characters in Act I.

Mr. *STEWART.*

Mr. *MAITLAND.*

Mr. *MACBEAN.*

Mr. *LEVETT.*

Dr. *JOHNSON.*

A VOICE (MacPherson's).

Mr. *BOSWELL.*

A SERVANT (Lord Chesterfield's).

Mrs. *WILLIAMS.*

FRANK (Dr. Johnson's Colored Servant).

Mr. *ALLEN.*

Mrs. *WOFFINGTON.*

BET FLINT.

POLL CARMICHAEL.

Mrs. *THRALE.*

Dr. *Johnson*.

ACT I.

We are in London in February 1755: in a house in Gough Square off Fleet Street. The attic in which we find ourselves, in which we can see and hear without being, ourselves, observed, is large with the ceiling sloping on one side. The sun shining obscurely through three windows suggests early dawn, but it is almost noon. Before each window is a small deal table; seated at these tables are three men, shabbily dressed; one is reading, the other two are writing. On the right a door opens into a passage. On the left a door opens into a bedroom. In a tiny grate in the corner a small fire burns, unwillingly. A screen in another corner partly conceals a couch on which is a man seemingly asleep. A very large deal table is in the centre of the room, in front of which is a great armchair, vacant. Plain shelves, loaded down with books, are on either side of each door. Folio volumes are in piles upon the floor. Extreme poverty is suggested in every detail. Papers are strewn about in great disorder. There is complete silence; finally one man, having finished his writing, sands it, sticks his quill behind his ear, gets up, stretches himself, and remarks: —

Mr. *STEWART*.

DR. JOHNSON is late this morning.

Mr. *MAITLAND*.

[*Putting down his book.*] Dr. Johnson is always late.

Mr. *STEWART*.

Mr. *STEWART*.

Dr. Johnson is later than usual.

Mr. *MAITLAND*.

Dr. Johnson is always later than usual.

Mr. *MACBEAN*.

[*Looking up from his writing*.] I suppose he feels that he can permit himself a little relaxation now that our dictionary is completed.

Mr. *STEWART*.

Our dictionary! You grammatical outcast; you had very little to do with it. Dr. Johnson only took you on from pity. [*After a pause*.] I feel that I have never done anything but copy, copy, copy: words, words, words. I'm not fit for anything else.

Mr. *MAITLAND*.

I well remember the time when Dr. Johnson thought you were not fit for that.

Mr. *STEWART*.

What do you mean?

Mr. *MAITLAND*.

That time when you copied letter "S" complete and entire on both sides of the paper and it had all to be done over again.

Mr. *MACBEAN*.

I remember, at a cost of twenty pounds. I expected to see Dr. Johnson lose his temper.

Mr. *MAITLAND*.

Mr. *MAITLAND*.

Instead of which he only remarked, Mistakes will happen: that which can be remedied at the expenditure of a few guineas cannot be regarded as serious. We must set doggedly to work and do it over again.

Mr. *MACBEAN*.

I am told that the money he was to receive from the book-sellers has all been spent.

Mr. *MAITLAND*.

Every penny of it, — and what we are to do now I can't imagine. Already I'm beginning to feel the pangs of hunger. I'll go and look for food.

Mr. *LEVETT*.

[*An awkward and uncouth old man, rising from the couch.*] Did I hear the word "food"?

Mr. *MAITLAND*.

You did; and hearing about it is as near as you're likely to come to breakfasting this morning. We eat every crumb in the house hours ago.

Mr. *LEVETT*.

Ah, well, I supped late last night and can fast till dinner. A grateful patient would insist upon my keeping him company till late, and as my day's work was done, I obliged him.

Mr. *MACBEAN*.

Mr. *MACBEAN*.

And in that way made sure of your fee, I suppose?

Mr. *LEVETT*.

I practise my profession for the love of it rather than for six-
pences. It makes little difference to me whether I am paid in
money or in food. Dr. Johnson gives me shelter here, and I
need little else.

Mr. *MACBEAN*.

And Mrs. Levett, what of her?

Mr. *LEVETT*.

What of her! Sir, mine was not the first unfortunate alliance.
Mrs. Levett still makes her living in the streets, as she was
accustomed to do before I married her. At present she is in
a jail. I hear that she is soon to be tried at the Old Bailey
for picking pockets. She may be transported unless I can per-
suade Dr. Johnson to speak for her character.

Mr. *MAITLAND*.

Which I have no doubt you can. To be in misery and distress is to be certain of Dr. Johnson's compassion. Did he
not testify as to the character of Mr. Thrale's tutor—what
was that Italian's name?

Mr. *LEVETT*.

Baretti; and he committed murder. He stabbed a man in the
street.

Mr. *MACBEAN*.

Mr. *MACBEAN.*

But under great provocation; in self-defense.

[*A street door closes with a bang and voices are heard outside.*]

Dr. *JOHNSON.*

[*In a loud voice.*] Retract! Sir, what would you have me retract? I thought your book an imposture, I think it an imposture still. Your rage I defy. I hope I shall never be deterred from detecting what I think a cheat by the menaces of a ruff—

A VOICE (MACPHERSON'S).

[*Outside.*] No man shall call me cheat and go unpunished.

Dr. *JOHNSON.*

Any violence offered me I shall do my best to repel, and what I cannot do for myself, the law shall do for me. Go, sir, and tell your friends of our quarrel.

Dr. JOHNSON, *a large, burly man, shabbily dressed, throws open the door and enters, followed by* JAMES BOSWELL, *a young man with a tiptilted nose, stylishly dressed.*

Mr. *BOSWELL.*

I am astonished—

Dr. *JOHNSON.*

Sir! you may be astonished, but your astonishment will be as nothing compared to the amazement of that scoundrel should he venture to attack me. I know how to take care of myself. Sam Foote once announced that he would take me off, as the

saying

saying goes, on the stage. I had the story from Tom Davies, the bookseller. What is the price of an oak stick, said I. Sixpence, said Tom. Give me leave, sir, said I, to send your servant to buy me a shilling's worth, I'll have double quantity and be ready for Mr. Foote's mimicry, and I give you leave to tell him so. Mr. Foote took his talents to another market. Good morning, Levett. Good morning, Gentlemen, our task is almost at an end; have our last sheets gone to the printer?

Mr. *STEWART.*

Yes, sir; Millar's messenger carried the last sheet away an hour since.

Dr. *JOHNSON.*

What did he say? Did he leave any message?

Mr. *STEWART.*

Yes, sir, he said: "Thank God I have done with him!"

Dr. *JOHNSON.*

[*Smiling benignly.*] I am glad he thanks God for anything. Gentlemen, shall we make it a holiday? You are excused until next Monday. At the Cheshire Cheese, near by in Fleet Street, there is beefsteak and kidney pie—and a mug of Mr. Thrale's ale. [*Giving Mr. Macbean a coin.*] Spend this among you.

Mr. *MACBEAN.*

Thank you, sir.

Mr. *STEWART.*

And I thank you, sir; good morning, sir.

Mr. *MAITLAND.*

Mr. *MAITLAND*.

[*Bowing.*] You are very good, sir.   [*The three leave the room.*

Mr. *BOSWELL*.

You must be relieved that the work is finished; you did not fully realize what you were undertaking when you set out.

Dr. *JOHNSON*.

Sir, I knew very well what I was undertaking and very well how to go about it,—and have done it very well,—but I sadly underestimated the time. It has taken me eight years.

Mr. *BOSWELL*.

But, sir, the French Academy, which consists of forty members, took forty years to compile their dictionary.

Dr. *JOHNSON*.

[*Smiling.*] Then, sir, this is the proportion. Let me see, forty times forty is sixteen hundred; as eight is to sixteen hundred, so is the proportion of an Englishman to a Frenchman.

Mr. *BOSWELL*.

I hope, sir, it has made you rich.

Dr. *JOHNSON*.

Sir, I did not work for money but for the honour of my country, that we might no longer yield the palm of philology to the nations of the Continent without a contest. I am, sir, in

point

point of fact, as poor as I have ever been. I would not say poorer, for that would be impossible. Indeed, only a few days ago I was arrested for debt.

Mr. *BOSWELL.*

Is it possible?

Dr. *JOHNSON.*

It is not unusual for an author to be arrested for debt; but the matter occasioned me little distress. Mr. Richardson became my surety and the matter was speedily adjusted.

Mr. *BOSWELL.*

But the booksellers! Surely, sir, they would not see you in want now that you have delivered to them so valuable a property.

Dr. *JOHNSON.*

Sir, they have treated me very well; they are generous, liberal-minded men, who have done all that they agreed to do. My chief concern is that I have protracted my work till most of those I wished to please have sunk into the grave. *Success* and *miscarriage* are now but empty words. I dismiss the result with frigid tranquillity, having little to fear from censure or to hope from praise.

Mr. *BOSWELL.*

But Lord Chesterfield! I am told that he has written a paper to *The World* in which he praises your work *in excelsis* and declares that he makes a total surrender of all his rights and privileges in the English language for the term of your dictatorship;

JAMES BOSWELL

From a Drawing by George Dance

tatorship; nay more, that he believes in you as his Pope and holds you to be infallible.

There is a loud rap upon the door which, before Dr. Johnson can reach it, is opened from the outside and a Young Man *in the livery of Lord Chesterfield enters. He carries himself with impudence and keeps his hat upon his head.*

SERVANT.

I have a letter from Lord Chesterfield for Dr. Johnson; there is an answer.

Dr. JOHNSON.

[*Taking the letter and twirling it in his hands, addressing himself slowly to Mr. Boswell.*] If my servant were here, I would tell him to inform that young monkey that if he did not remove his hat I should be under the necessity of throwing him down the staircase; as it is, I shall be obliged to do so — without warning. [*Instantly the hat comes off and the servant is all politeness.*]

SERVANT.

Beg pardon, sir; I'm very sorry, sir; I did not know Dr. Johnson was in the room. Will you read the letter, sir? There is an answer, sir.

Dr. JOHNSON.

[*Opening the letter, reads aloud.*] Lord Chesterfield presents his compliments to Dr. Johnson and takes this method of informing him that the dedication of the Dictionary will not be be displeasing to him, and that he is ready to show his appreciation in whatever manner will be agreeable to its distinguished author.

Mr. *BOSWELL.*

Very handsomely said.

Dr. *JOHNSON.*

Why, no, sir, it is too late. I am indifferent as to what he may say and unwilling to confess obligation where no benefit has been received. I would not have the public believe that I owe to him that which Providence has enabled me to do by myself.

Mr. *BOSWELL.*

Lord Chesterfield is a very proud man, but you are, I think, the prouder man of the two.

Dr. *JOHNSON.*

Mine, sir, is defensive pride. But enough of this. [*To the servant.*] Tell your master that there is no answer: that I will communicate with him.

SERVANT.

Thank you, sir. [*He goes.*

Dr. *JOHNSON.*

[*To* LEVETT.] Where is Frank?

Mr. *LEVETT.*

He was here, sir, not long since. He has, I think, gone on an errand for Mrs. Williams.

Dr. *JOHNSON.*

Dr. *JOHNSON.*

Ah, the dear lady. I hope she wants for nothing.

Mr. *LEVETT.*

I think not, sir. If I am not mistaken, she sent him for some cat's meat for "Hodge."

Dr. *JOHNSON.*

I am sorry for that; she should have waited until my return: I would have gone for it. I much dislike having a servant wait upon an animal. Hodge is a good cat, but is — nevertheless — a cat.

Enter Mrs. WILLIAMS, *who is blind and a trifle deaf.*

Mrs. *WILLIAMS.*

Did I hear some one say I was a cat?

Dr. *JOHNSON.*

Not in my hearing, madam; we were speaking of the wants of Hodge.

Mrs. *WILLIAMS.*

Ah, yes. I sent Frank for some cat's meat — he should be back by this time.

Dr. *JOHNSON.*

When he comes will you give him this penny? [*Handing Mrs. Williams a coin.*] I would not have him feel put upon, as the saying is, by going errands for a cat.

Mr. *BOSWELL.*

Mr. *BOSWELL.*

You do not, sir, always treat your friends with so much consideration.

Dr. *JOHNSON.*

My friends, sir, know how to protect themselves. Consideration for one's servants is the hallmark of the gentleman.

Mr. *BOSWELL.*

I shall remember this. Dr. Johnson, have you seen the epigram of Mr. Garrick on your Dictionary? It is prodigiously clever.

Dr. *JOHNSON.*

Sir, do not use large words for small matters. It is, I grant you, complimentary coming from an old pupil, but Davy is not much of a poet: he is always endeavouring to shine out of his line. He should confine himself to the stage, where he has few equals and no superiors.

Mr. *BOSWELL.*

I think the couplet,

> "*And Johnson, well arm'd, like a hero of yore*
> *Has beat forty French, and will beat forty more!*"

excellent.

Dr. *JOHNSON.*

Sir, you may think it excellent, but that does not make it so.

A COLORED SERVANT *enters.*

But here comes my faithful servant. Frank, I am expecting a visit from a French lady of great distinction; should she call

call to-day, admit her with all ceremony: we must not let the French outdo us in politeness.

FRANK.

Yes, master. *[He bows and retires.*

Mr. *LEVETT.*

Dr. Johnson, may I have a word with you? My wife occasions me much concern. I have been arrested for debts of her contracting, she spends much of her time in the streets, and I hear that she is to be tried at the Old Bailey for picking pockets, unless, sir, you will stand for her character.

Dr. *JOHNSON.*

I! Sir, you amaze me. I have not been without suspicion that you have been cheated in your wife, but this is a matter in which your friends can be of little service. I would not be a slave to her caprice. It might be for the best that she should be sent to the Plantations.

Mr. *LEVETT.*

Sir, sometimes I think it would.

Dr. *JOHNSON.*

A man should marry for virtue, for wit, for beauty, or for money. I cannot see that you have secured these or any of them by the surrender of your independence. I suggest that the law take its course. You shall make your home with me. Mrs. Williams shall look after your wants, and Poll Carmichael

chael shall so hector you that you will think your lady has returned.

Mr. *LEVETT.*

I have no doubt she will, sir.   [*Mr.* LEVETT *leaves the room.*

Dr. *JOHNSON.*

He married a streetwalker who had persuaded him that she was nearly related to a man of fortune: she regarded him as a physician in considerable practice. The marvels of the alliance make commonplace the occurrences of the Arabian Nights.

Mr. *BOSWELL.*

But, sir, who is Poll Carmichael?

Dr. *JOHNSON.*

Why, sir, I am not sure that I know. She is a poor woman of violent temper that I picked up one night in the street, desperately ill: and I brought her here on my back. In short, sir, she is a slut, but she has no home and I took her in.

Enter FRANK.

FRANK.

Dr. Johnson, Mr. Allen craves a dozen words with you, sir, on a subject, he says, of the greatest importance.

Dr. *JOHNSON.*

Tell him to come up. [*To Mr. Boswell.*] Mr. Allen is my neighbour and landlord, and an excellent man: his dinners, too, are excellent.

Enter

Enter Mr. ALLEN.

Mr. *ALLEN.*

Dr. Johnson, excuse my thus interrupting you in your study, but my friend Dr. Dodd, the unfortunate clergyman, has been sentenced to be hanged for forgery. [*Discovering Mr. Boswell.*] Pardon me, sir, I did not know that you were engaged.

Dr. *JOHNSON.*

Mr. James Boswell, Mr. Allen, and a very good friend of mine. [*They shake hands.*] Can I be of any service to your friend? Dr. Dodd to be hanged! A clergyman! This is awful!

Mr. *ALLEN.*

It is thought, sir, that you can do much. His friends would petition the Lord Chancellor, the King even, for a pardon or a commutation of the sentence. Signatures can be had by thousands.

Dr. *JOHNSON.*

I do not doubt it. People will put their name to anything, chiefly for the satisfaction of showing that they can write. But what is my part? I am expected to prepare the petition, I suppose?

Mr. *ALLEN.*

If you will be so good.

Dr. *JOHNSON.*

I must first make myself acquainted with the facts. I would not wish to be known as moving in the matter, but will do
what

what I can. There has never been a time when the thought
of death was not terrible to me.

Mr. *BOSWELL.*

I, too, have given much thought to the subject of death.

Dr. *JOHNSON.*

Sir, let us not discuss it; it matters not so much how a man
dies but how he lives.

Mr. *ALLEN.*

I thank you, sir, and will go at once to Dr. Dodd. I have in-
fluence with Mr. Ackerman, the keeper at Newgate. I bid you
good day, sir. Mr. Boswell, your very obedient.   [*He goes out.*

Mr. *BOSWELL.*

Is Dr. Dodd a friend of yours, sir?

Dr. *JOHNSON.*

No, sir. I saw him once, I think.

Mr. *BOSWELL.*

Then why this distress on his account?

Dr. *JOHNSON.*

He is a human being: is not that enough?

Mr. *BOSWELL.*

He was, I have heard, a very bad man.

Dr. *JOHNSON.*

Dr. *JOHNSON*.

Sir, he may have been, but the worst man does more good than evil: he is a friend of Allen's, who is a friend of mine, and he is a clergyman.

Mr. *BOSWELL*.

You have many friends, sir.

Dr. *JOHNSON*.

I hope I have, sir; if a man does not make new acquaintances as he advances through life, he will soon find himself alone. A man, sir, should keep his friendships in constant repair.

Enter FRANK.

FRANK.

[*Announcing with a flourish*.] The lady from France.

Enter Mrs. WOFFINGTON.

Dr. *JOHNSON*.

My dear Peg!

Mrs. *WOFFINGTON*.

Why all this ceremony? You cannot, sir, have been expecting to see me.

Dr. *JOHNSON*.

No, madam, but I had an inkling of a visit from Madame de Boufflers, a French lady of wit and fashion, and I had instructed my man to be very polite, as I would not seem un-
                                                    appreciative

appreciative of her call. Permit me, madam, to present Mr.
James Boswell, a young gentleman just come from Scotland.

Mr. *BOSWELL.*

Your very humble servant, madam. I only arrived yesterday
and have not yet had the unspeakable delight of seeing you,
tho' your fame has reached us in the north. In what part are
you now ravishing the town?

Mrs. *WOFFINGTON.*

As Sir Harry Wildair; sir, the town is good enough—

Mr. *BOSWELL.*

I join the ranks of your adorers, madam, and shall not drink
wine till I have seen you.

Dr. *JOHNSON.*

But, madam, to what do I owe the honour of this call?

Mrs. *WOFFINGTON.*

I am almost ashamed to tell you, sir, but I heard that a gentleman was with you, sir, and I thought he might be Davy, sir.
We have had a quarrel and he has left me—and I much fear
for Kitty Fisher.

Mr. *BOSWELL.*

Oh, madam, he will return, or if he does not, I—

Dr. *JOHNSON.*

Silence, sir! I will not have you make an assignation in my
house. [*To Mrs. Woffington.*] Depend upon it, madam, Davy
will

will soon return; when he does, let me know and I will drop in and have a cup of tea with you—strong tea, madam, of your making.

Mrs. *WOFFINGTON.*

You have been such a comfort to me. I could not, I think, live without Davy. Gentlemen, [*with a low bow*] I bid you good day.   [*She goes out.*

Mr. *BOSWELL.*

How delightful she is!

Dr. *JOHNSON.*

Why yes, sir, one does not commonly take the town by storm without uncommon charm. But I hope Garrick has not gone to Kitty Fisher, else I shall have another friend in distress.

Mr. *BOSWELL.*

And who may that be?

Dr. *JOHNSON.*

Why, from the number of portraits he has made of her, I rather think Sir Joshua Reynolds is taken in that quarter.

Mr. *BOSWELL.*

I assure you, sir, he would soon recover from the blow. I remember to have had my heart broken twice—within six months—by the desertion of a mistress. Oh, how delighted I am to be in London again! I thought that my coach would never arrive. Fleet Street, I think, never had so animated an appearance.

Dr. *JOHNSON.*

Dr. *JOHNSON.*

It has, sir; but the high tide of human existence is, I think, at Charing Cross.

The passage door opens very quietly and BET FLINT, *a woman of the town, enters.*

Bet! I am surprised to see you.

BET FLINT.

I knew you would be, sir, but I have come to ask a favour of you, sir: I have written my life in verse and the publishers say it would have a greater sale if you were to write an introduction to it.

Dr. *JOHNSON.*

Why, Bet, no doubt it would, but I can hardly do that. What would the newspapers say? They are always telling lies about us old fellows. No, my girl, it won't do. Take your verses to some of your admirers, you have enough.

BET FLINT.

Yes, sir, surely, sir, but I wanted Dr. Johnson —

Dr. *JOHNSON.*

And I would oblige you if I could, but it is impossible. Run along — [*with a smile*] I was just about to say, there's a good girl. [*He sees her to the door. James Boswell seems to be attracted by her.*]

Mr. *BOSWELL.*

And pray, sir, who may that be?

Dr. *JOHNSON.*

Dr. *JOHNSON.*

Bet Flint. I am glad that you do not know her: she is
habitually a drunkard and a woman of the town, occasionally
a thief, needless to say a woman of much effrontery — from
the country, I think.

Mr. *BOSWELL.*

London draws all kinds to itself. Country girls come to town
to conceal their shame, and men of learning to meet their
match.

Dr. *JOHNSON.*

They do, sir; people who live in the country are fit for the
country. There is, I think, within ten miles from where we
are now sitting, more learning than in all the rest of England
— aye, and Scotland, too, sir — put together.

Mr. *BOSWELL.*

Sir, that reminds me of a question I wished to ask. Have
you received any assistance from the learned in the compi-
lation of your great Dictionary?

Dr. *JOHNSON.*

If I may except twenty etymologies, sent me anonymously
by a gentleman whom I afterwards discovered to be the
Bishop of Rochester, I laboured alone: not in the soft ob-
scurities of retirement or under the shelter of academic
bowers, but amidst inconvenience and distraction, in poverty, in sickness, and in sorrow.

Mr. *BOSWELL.*

Mr. *BOSWELL*.

Yet, sir, you shall have your reward: to have grappled single-handed with great libraries; surely your name will last as long as the language you have done so much to perpetuate.

Dr. *JOHNSON*.

Sir, I was a poet doomed at last to awake a lexicographer. The unhappy writer of a dictionary labours without hope of praise, fortunate if he escapes reproach, but I am not yet so lost in lexicography as to forget that words are the daughters of earth and that things are the sons of heaven.

Mr. *BOSWELL*.

Lord Chesterfield will be much chagrined if you do not dedicate your work to him.

Dr. *JOHNSON*.

Sir, after making great professions he ignored me. It is seven years since I waited in his outward rooms, during which time I brought my work to completion without one act of assistance, one word of encouragement, or one smile of favour. The notice which he is now pleased to take of my labours, had it been early, had been kind; but it has been delayed till I am indifferent, and cannot enjoy it; till I am solitary and cannot impart it; till I am known and do not want it. I once thought him a Lord among wits, but I find he is only a wit among Lords. The chief glory of a nation is its people, and to them I shall dedicate my work.

Mr. *BOSWELL*.

Mr. *BOSWELL*.

Would it not be curious, sir, taking into consideration your dislike of the Scotch and your contempt for Presbyterians, if a century or so from now the Oxford University Press decided to bring out an edition of your Dictionary edited by a Scotch Presbyterian?

Dr. *JOHNSON*.

[*Savagely*.] To be facetious, sir, it is not necessary to be indecent.

Enter POLL CARMICHAEL.

What is it, Poll?

POLL *CARMICHAEL*.

Dr. Johnson, I cannot well manage the roast for we have no jack.

Dr. *JOHNSON*.

Do the best you can with a string, my dear. [*To Boswell*.] I have for some time contemplated buying a jack because I think a jack is some credit to a house.   [*She goes out*.

Mr. *BOSWELL*.

Well, but you'll have a spit, too?

Dr. *JOHNSON*.

No, sir, no; that would be superfluous, for we should never use it; if a jack is seen, a spit will be presumed.

Enter

Enter FRANK.

FRANK.

Another lady, sir, to see you. She would not give her name.

Dr. *JOHNSON.*

Madame de Boufflers, at last! Frank could not manage the name. Ask her to have the kindness to ascend. Quick, sir, take this chair and be careful, it has but three legs. My lady from France must have the only sound chair in the room. [*Places a sound chair conspicuously.*]

Enter Mrs. THRALE.

Mrs. *THRALE.*

Dr. Johnson, Mr. Boswell, you were, it appears, expecting me.

Dr. *JOHNSON.*

Not you, madam, but a French lady of distinction, hence these preparations. But you are welcome. Be seated, madam; cast yourself into the arms of this chair in all confidence; they are sound—as are also its legs.

Mrs. *THRALE.*

I do not hesitate to accept your invitation, but I must get to business before interruption. I am come, sir, to carry you with me to the country.

Dr. *JOHNSON.*

To the country, madam! Why should you carry me to the country?

Mrs. *THRALE.*

MRS. THRALE

From a Drawing by George Dance

Mrs. *THRALE*.

Change of scene and change of air, change of company and change of food. You have been caged up here with this menagerie of yours all too long. Mr. Thrale charged me not to return to Streatham without you.

Dr. *JOHNSON*.

It is most kind of you, madam, but I cannot go. I have undertaken certain duties that I would fain perform.

Mrs. *THRALE*.

Mr. Boswell we could take with us.

Mr. *BOSWELL*.

Your most obedient, madam. In your company and in Dr. Johnson's I could be happy on a desert island.

Mrs. *THRALE*.

And Streatham is not a desert island. My coach and four awaits us in Fleet Street. In an hour you shall have exchanged the bricks and mortar of London for fresh fields and pastures new.

Dr. *JOHNSON*.

[*Correcting her.*] Fresh *woods* and pastures new, madam. It is in "Lycidas," but the sentiment does not appeal to me; one green field is like another, and the same may be said of a woods.

Mrs. *THRALE*.

But surely you do not enjoy the sordid sights and stenches of the town?

Dr. *JOHNSON*.

Dr. *JOHNSON*.

Not all the sights of London are sordid, many are magnificent; and as for its smells — [*blowing hard*] pooh!

Mrs. *THRALE*.

We have a fine library at Streatham. I have just received a parcel of new books as to which I want your opinion, and Mr. Thrale will, I am sure, wish to discuss with you the merits of a dish of lampreys he has just received from Scotland; our strawberries grown under glass are just coming in; fancy! strawberries and clotted cream so early in the season —and in profusion, too!

Dr. *JOHNSON*.

Madam, you would shake the resolution of a much stronger man than I am. But only a moment ago Poll Carmichael was here telling me of a roast that we were to have for dinner, and Mrs. Williams and Desmoulins and Levett. They all hate one another; I alone can order sufficient tranquillity to enable every member of my menagerie, as you call it, to eat their dinner in peace: it was to be a dinner in honour of the completion of my Dictionary.

Mrs. *THRALE*.

You may argue, sir, but I will not be denied. Let me reason with Mrs. Williams, the only one of your family group susceptible to reason. She will admit that now your great book is finished you should allow yourself a little relaxation. And
consider,

consider, sir, the fewer the mouths, the greater the quantity of food to go into them. What you do not eat will, no doubt, be cheerfully consumed by the hungry-looking individual I passed upon the staircase.

Dr. *JOHNSON.*

I had thought to have dined at home, and there is the possibility of a charming woman from France—

Mrs. *THRALE.*

Let no possibility of a charming woman from France keep you from enjoying the actuality of a [*with a curtsy*] charming woman from Wales. And there is a good dinner to be eaten; although I lead the life of a kept woman, I am not altogether deprived of the confidence of our cook, and before I left home this morning I swore not only that I would be home in time for it, but that I would fetch with me the Great Lexicographer. Preparations are now going forward; in imagination I smell a turtle soup,—and the lampreys are fresh from Scotland, there is a saddle of lamb, fresh peas, and sparrowgrass, and veal pie with raisins in it—

Dr. *JOHNSON.*

Enough, madam, enough, a feast for Lucullus.

Mrs. *THRALE.*

—A tender ham, and the glass houses of Streatham are famous for their fruits. It is too early for walled fruit, but the fragrance of the pineapples is delicious, and the oranges were

were superb when I last saw them. Mr. Thrale drinks wine and perhaps you can be tempted to keep him company, or should you prefer it, join me in lemonade.

Dr. *JOHNSON*.

My resolution is like snow in the sun. It is a dinner to ask a man to. Some people pretend not to mind what they eat: for my part I mind my belly very studiously; he who does not will hardly mind anything else. Mr. Boswell will excuse me, I am sure. [*In a loud voice.*] Frank, a clean shirt! I'm for the country!

Enter FRANK.

FRANK.

[*Bowing and smiling.*] Yes, sir, yes, sir.

Act II.

Characters in Act II.

Mrs. *THRALE.*

JUDSON.

RATTLE.

Miss *BURNEY.*

Mr. *MURPHY.*

Sir *JOSHUA REYNOLDS.*

Mr. *GARRICK.*

Mrs. *GARRICK.*

Dr. *JOHNSON.*

Mr. *THRALE.*

Dr. *GOLDSMITH.*

General *PAOLI.*

Mr. *BOSWELL.*

Miss *MORE.*

Mr. *PIOZZI.*

Mrs. *CARTER.*

Miss *STREATFIELD.*

Mrs. *DELANEY.*

Mr. *BARETTI.*

ACT II.

The drawing-room at Streatham, a large country house a few miles from London. Upon the walls are fine portraits, of Dr. Johnson, Henry and Mrs. Thrale, Fanny Burney, Garrick, Goldsmith, and others, from the brush of Reynolds. Windows to the floor open upon a park of great beauty; under the trees deer may be seen. It is afternoon. Double doors, closed, to the left open into a large dining-room; double doors to the right, open, reveal a large comfortably furnished hall. Everything suggests comfort rather than magnificence, although evidences of wealth are not lacking. There is a large table filled with books, comfortable chairs abound, tall vases are filled with flowers, heavy silver candlesticks are conveniently placed; from the ceiling are suspended two large crystal lustres containing innumerable wax candles. Some years have passed since Dr. Johnson first visited the Thrales, with whom he now spends most of his time, although he still maintains lodgings in London. Mrs. THRALE enters followed by JUDSON, a footman, to inspect the room, for a formal dinner party will soon be in progress.

Mrs. *THRALE.*

JUDSON, see that Dr. Johnson is presentable when he comes down, that he wears his best suit, his shoes with silver buckles, and his new wig. Be particular about the wig, his old one is so singed from the candles that it must be discarded; lose it, forever, somewhere.

JUDSON.

Yes, ma'am.

Mrs. *THRALE.*

Mr. Thrale has ordered the wine? What have we?

JUDSON.

JUDSON.

Hock, claret, port, and brandy, ma'am.

Mrs. *THRALE.*

Have vast quantities of tea and lemonade also, for Dr. Johnson.

JUDSON.

Yes, ma'am.

Mrs. *THRALE.*

Send Rattle to me.

JUDSON.

Yes, ma'am.   [*He goes out.*

Mrs. *THRALE.*

[*Giving a tug at a great bunch of roses. To herself.*] Who could have supposed that I, the wife of a rich brewer, would be entertaining at dinner the most distinguished company in London?

Enter RATTLE.

RATTLE.

You sent for me, ma'am?

Mrs. *THRALE.*

See if Miss Burney wants anything and tell her I await her in the drawing-room; then tell Miss Streatfield where I am. [*To herself.*] She shall shed tears for us after dinner; it will amuse Mr. Thrale, who is in low spirits.

RATTLE.

Yes, ma'am.   [*She goes out.*

Mrs. *THRALE.*

Mrs. *THRALE*.

[*Taking up a book, which she discards as Miss* BURNEY *enters.*]
Oh, there you are, I have been awaiting you this hour or more.
What a pretty frock! Dr. Johnson will be pleased. He always notices what ladies wear in spite of the fact that he is
almost blind. He once said to me, Why are you dressed in
that evil-looking gown? go to your room and change it.
Women, like butterflies, should always wear gay colours.

Miss *BURNEY*.

Oh, if Dr. Johnson should speak so to me, I would swoon.
Ten to one he will not know I am in the room.

Mrs. *THRALE*.

Wait and see, my dear. Dr. Johnson is eager to make the acquaintance of the author of *Evelina*.

Miss *BURNEY*.

I hope the room may be crowded when he enters, that I may
escape unnoticed.

Mrs. *THRALE*.

Dr. Johnson would be here now if he suspected you were in
the room: he is always the first at any function.

Footman announces Mr. MURPHY, *who enters.*

Oh, Mr. Murphy, so pleased.

Mr. *MURPHY*.

Your servant, madam. [*Steps to one side.*]

Footman

Footman announces Sir JOSHUA REYNOLDS, *who enters, carrying an ear trumpet.*

Mrs. *THRALE*.

Oh, dear Sir Joshua, how good of you! But you come, I am sure, not so much to see us as to see Miss Burney here, the author of *Evelina*.

Sir *JOSHUA*.

[*Bowing and shaking hands.*] Is she here? The prodigy! I laid ten guineas that the author was a man about town of my acquaintance, and now it turns out the book which is the talk of all London was written by the daughter of my old friend and present neighbour, Dr. Burney. We live in amazing times.

Mrs. *THRALE*.

Let me present you. Come, my dear Miss Burney, and meet two admirers: Sir Joshua Reynolds, who has known you all of your young life, and Mr. Murphy, who no doubt will soon be teasing you to join him in writing a comedy. He says such wit and such power of observation as you display cannot fail to take the town by storm. He is already revolving in his mind a plot.

Miss *BURNEY*.

Oh, madam, oh, sir, do not mention it, I beg of you. My father is greatly shocked that I should have written a novel: judge of his feelings should he hear that I, whose knowledge of the world is chiefly gathered from conversations overheard in our drawing-room, was engaged upon a comedy.

Footman

Footman announces Mr. and Mrs. Garrick.

Mr. *GARRICK.*

[*Rather stiltedly,* "'*Twas only when off the stage he was acting.*"]
Madam, your most obedient.

Mrs. *THRALE.*

So very good of you, Mr. Garrick, and Mrs. Garrick, too —
So very pleased. [*They shake hands.*] I hope you did not find
the journey from town tedious. The roads are so dusty at this
season. I was saying to Dr. Johnson only an hour ago —

Footman announces Dr. Johnson, *who at once goes up to Mr.
Garrick.*

Dr. *JOHNSON.*

Well, Davy, in what are you exhibiting yourself now?

Mr. *GARRICK.*

[*Somewhat nettled.*] Sir, I am playing, and I may say with
some success, Richard the Third.

Dr. *JOHNSON.*

[*Laughing vociferously.*] The fellow claps a hump on his back
and a lump on his leg, and cries, "I am Richard the Third."
It won't do, Davy, it won't do.

Mr. *GARRICK.*

I beg to assure you, sir, it will do very well; the house is
crowded every night.

Dr. *JOHNSON.*

Dr. *JOHNSON*.

Nay, sir. A crowded house means nothing. People will crowd a house to see a dog walking on its hind legs. [*Walks away.*]

Mr. *THRALE*.

[*Who has entered the drawing-room unobserved.*] Mr. Garrick, in the words of Jonson, Ben, not Sam:—

> "*To-night, good sir, both my poor house and I*
> *Do equally desire your company;*
> *Not that we think us worthy such a guest,*
> *But that your worth will dignify our feast.*"

You must forgive Dr. Johnson his rudeness, which is indeed only a cloak for his regard; he will permit no one to abuse you but himself.

Mr. *GARRICK*.

So I have often been told. I was once his pupil; we came to London together, penniless. I gave the town what it wanted: he, what it deserved. I have had applause; he, "toil, envy, want, the garret and the jail." But, sir, Dr. Goldsmith has said the last word concerning him. There is nothing of the bear about him but its skin.

Mr. *THRALE*.

I would add, its claws also, but I am taming him.

Footman announces Dr. GOLDSMITH.

I am glad to see you; we were just speaking of you. [*They shake hands.*]

Dr. *GOLDSMITH*.

OLIVER GOLDSMITH
From a Sketch by Sir Joshua Reynolds

Dr. *GOLDSMITH*.

Nothing to my disadvantage, I hope; certainly my apparel is beyond criticism. I have just had this suit from my tailor. You will agree, I think, that this plum colour is most unusual, most becoming.

Mr. *GARRICK*.

It is unusual, certainly. Where did you get it?

Dr. *GOLDSMITH*.

From John Filby at the Sign of the Harrow in Water Lane. I promised to mention it. I think he would be much honoured if you would call upon him.

Mr. *GARRICK*.

I am quite sure of it. But you have the advantage of me in figure; your fine form sets off Mr. Filby's clothes to great advantage.

Dr. *GOLDSMITH*.

Just what I observed to Filby. I am glad that we agree, — great minds, — you take me, sir! But there is Dr. Johnson. I must show myself to him.

Dr. *JOHNSON*.

Ah! Goldy, I am glad to see you. The play still goes well, I hear, and it deserves to; no comedy in many years has so much exhilarated an audience; has so well answered the end of comedy — that of making an audience merry. I am, sir, much honoured by the dedication.

Dr. *GOLDSMITH*.

Dr. *GOLDSMITH*.

Sir, it does me honour to inform the public that I have lived for many years in intimacy with you. I meant not so much to compliment you as myself.

Dr. *JOHNSON*.

Very handsomely said; but here we are bandying words with one another when we should be paying compliments to a young lady who has just begun to browse upon the literary common. You have met the daughter of my friend, Dr. Burney? Fanny, a shy little dunce we thought her. Sir, she has written an excellent novel of London life and character. I never read a better.

Dr. *GOLDSMITH*.

That is praise indeed, and curiously enough a day or two ago when I met Sir Joshua he told me of a novel he had just been reading, a novel published anonymously by Lowndes, and which he said so intrigued him that he would give ten pounds to know the name of the author.

Dr. *JOHNSON*.

We are speaking of the same book, *Evelina*.

Dr. *GOLDSMITH*.

But, sir, how can that be? He called on Lowndes and was informed that the book in question was written by a gentleman at the other end of the town.

Dr. *JOHNSON*.

As Lowndes had every reason to suppose. But I assure you
                                                            Evelina

Evelina was written by Fanny Burney, my little Burney, she confessed to it not ten minutes since.

Dr. *GOLDSMITH.*

You must present me. I think I do not know the young lady.

Dr. *JOHNSON.*

With pleasure, sir. Direct your steps to the sofa at the other end of the room. I left her there in the company of Mrs. Garrick. [*They approach Miss Burney.*] The best dramatist and the best novelist of the age should be acquainted. Dr. Goldsmith, Miss Burney, the daughter of my old friend.

Miss *BURNEY.*

Oh, sir, this is the most consequential day of my life: to have Dr. Johnson mention me in the same breath with the author of *She Stoops to Conquer.* I wish that I might rise to the occasion, but my legs are all of a flutter. I do not deserve this honour.

Dr. *JOHNSON.*

Don't say so, my dear—the public to whom we authors make appeal has agreed that you are certainly wittier and probably wiser than the generality of your sex: rest satisfied with its opinion, it seldom errs.

Mrs. *THRALE.*

And a public which includes Dr. Johnson, Sir Joshua, and Mr. Burke among the men, and Mrs. Montagu, Elizabeth Carter, and Miss More among the women can hardly be in error.

Dr. *JOHNSON.*

Dr. *JOHNSON.*

Why, no, madam, it would seem not, but our Fanny must be prepared to bear with a little abuse by and by: she will not always be surrounded by her friends who love and flatter her. I would prepare her if I could to meet the world—

Mrs. *THRALE.*

By what means, sir? By flattery? My praise is a mere twitter compared with yours. Do you not agree, Dr. Goldsmith?

Dr. *GOLDSMITH.*

[*Who has been looking at himself in a mirror and has heard nothing of the conversation.*] I certainly do, madam. [*Turning to Dr. Johnson*] I am glad to see that Mr. Garrick is able to be out again, but do you not think, sir, that he is aging?

Dr. *JOHNSON.*

Why no, sir; you must remember that Garrick's face has had more wear and tear than any other man's, it is never at rest; such an eternal, restless, fatiguing play of the muscles must certainly wear out a man's face before its real time. Burney, my dear, I think I shall take a seat by your side.

Dr. *GOLDSMITH.*

I must speak to my host. He seems for the moment to be at leisure. Mr. Thrale, I hope I see you well, sir.

Mr. *THRALE.*

Indifferent well; we men of affairs have much to contend with which you literary fellows know nothing of.

Dr. *GOLDSMITH.*

Dr. *GOLDSMITH*.

And we literary fellows have little with which to contend with the world; but, sir, I see admiration in your glance. This suit from Filby, John Filby at the Harrow in Water Lane. Mr. Garrick has just observed that it sets off my figure to great advantage.

Mrs. *THRALE*.

[*Coming up and overhearing the conversation.*] And I'm sure no one has greater taste in dress than Mr. Garrick.

Mr. *GARRICK*.

Do I hear my name?

Mrs. *THRALE*.

You do, Mr. Garrick: I was just observing to Mr. Goldsmith that no one had ever played such a great variety of characters as yourself: that you excelled equally in comedy and in tragedy.

Dr. *GOLDSMITH*.

Although I have every reason to be satisfied with the success of my comedy, I am bitterly disappointed that Mr. Garrick could not see his way clear to the part of Tony Lumpkin.

Dr. *JOHNSON*.

[*Joining the party.*] Do you remember, sir, when we were all in labour for a title for the play? And how I suggested *The Mistakes of a Night* while you were insisting upon *She Stoops to Conquer?*

Dr. *GOLDSMITH*.

Dr. *GOLDSMITH*.

Yes, and for once I neglected to take your advice without living to regret it.

Footman announces General PAOLI *and Mr.* BOSWELL. *A large fine-looking man of distinguished bearing and Mr.* BOSWELL *enter. Mrs. Thrale welcomes the first effusively, and the latter with some reserve.*

Mrs. *THRALE*.

General, we are much honoured. Mr. Boswell, you see your hero with Dr. Goldsmith. Dr. Johnson has just been saying that if the selection of his biographer were left to him, he would undoubtedly select Dr. Goldsmith; that he has put his hand to every form of composition and has equally adorned them all.

Mr. *BOSWELL*.

[*Somewhat nettled.*] Except the biographical, madam; it is my set purpose to write the life of my revered friend. When it appears—and I hope that may not be for twenty years—it will be found to be the greatest biography that has ever been written. Have I not the greatest subject? I mean not only to give a history of Dr. Johnson's visible progress through the world, but a view of his mind—so far as it is within my power to do so.

Mrs. *THRALE*.

No doubt you will take his life with all skill; but here comes the great man, let us not appear to be talking about him.

Mr. *BOSWELL*.

GENERAL PAOLI

From a Drawing by George Dance

Mr. *BOSWELL.*

Good evening, Dr. Johnson, I hope I see you well after our dissipation of last night. I confess my head ached very considerably this morning.

Dr. *JOHNSON.*

Why, sir, I am not surprised to hear it. I have no objection to a man's drinking wine if he can do it in moderation. I cannot drink in moderation, therefore I never touch it. But, sir, it was not the wine that made your head ache but the sense that I put into it.

Mr. *BOSWELL.*

[*Thinking he has him.*] Why, Dr. Johnson, does sense make the head ache?

Dr. *JOHNSON.*

Yes, sir, when the head is not used to it.

General *PAOLI.*

[*Coming up and very respectfully saluting Dr. Johnson.*] Dr. Johnson, you are, I presume, inculcating lessons of sobriety and decorum upon our young friend here.

Dr. *JOHNSON.*

Why, sir, I am always doing so: with what effect you may judge.

Mr. *BOSWELL.*

But, sir, much may be said in favour of drinking: *in vino veritas*, you know.

Dr. *JOHNSON.*

Dr. *JOHNSON*.

I do. But I would not keep company with a man who lies when he is sober and whom you must make drunk before you can get a word of truth out of him. Drinking should be practised with great prudence: a man who exposes himself when he is intoxicated has not the art of getting drunk.

General *PAOLI*.

Dr. Johnson, you would, I am sure, recommend claret; one can drink a deal of claret without inconvenience.

Dr. *JOHNSON*.

Why no, sir, it is poor stuff: one can be drowned with claret before one feels the effect of it. Claret is the liquor for boys, port for men, and brandy for heroes. [*With a bow.*] You, General, would naturally drink brandy. Indeed, brandy will soonest do for a man what drinking can do for him.

Mr. *BOSWELL*.

[*Standing between Paoli and Johnson.*] I feel, gentlemen, like an isthmus uniting two great continents.

Dr. *JOHNSON*.

Which means, I take it, that your narrowness is apparent and your depth concealed. But there is Garrick, I said something a few minutes ago which nettled him. I must go and make it up with him. [*Walking up to him.*] Are you at your villa at Hampton? A charming place. When is your good lady going to ask me to drink a dish of tea with her?

Mr. *GARRICK*.

Mr. *GARRICK*.

I am sure that she will be honoured at your mentioning it, and I hope when you are next in the vicinity of Drury Lane you will look in on me in the greenroom.

Dr. *JOHNSON*.

No, Davy, I'll come no more behind your scenes; the silk stockings and white bosoms of your actresses excite my amorous propensities.

Footman announces Miss HANNAH MORE, *a slightly deaf old lady. Mrs. Thrale comes forward to receive her.*

Mrs. *THRALE*.

So very pleased; you did not come alone?

Miss *MORE*.

No, I came with dear Mrs. Delaney, who seeks a few moments' repose after the fatigue of the journey.

Mrs. *THRALE*.

Which was without incident, I hope?

Miss *MORE*.

Quite.

Dr. *JOHNSON*.

[*Talking to Mr. Garrick.*] I found him an insufferable prig.

Miss *MORE*.

Miss *MORE*.

[*Overhearing Dr. Johnson's remark.*] Did you say he was a Whig?

Dr. *JOHNSON*.

No, madam, I said he was a prig, but indeed he is both, prig and Whig.

Mr. *GARRICK*.

I, too, am a Whig. I wonder why you do not make me a Tory; you love to make people Tories.

Dr. *JOHNSON*.

[*Drawing some copper coins from his pocket.*] For the same reason that the King did not make these pence guineas: not the proper metal, sir. [*Mr. Garrick walks away in high dudgeon. Dr. Johnson turns to Mr. Boswell.*] Now I have offended him again, yet I love him. A game of jokes is composed partly of skill, partly of chance. A man may be beat at times by one who has not a tenth part of his wit. Davy is the first man in London for sprightly conversation.

Mr. *BOSWELL*.

And yet I have heard you abuse him. You were telling me only the other day of his having refused you an order for the play to the value of three shillings.

Dr. *JOHNSON*.

[*With a stern look.*] Sir, I have known David Garrick longer than you have, and I know no right you have to talk to me on the subject. Garrick was very poor when he began life,

and

and so when he came to have money he probably was unskill-
ful in giving it away and saved when he should not, but I
know that he has given away more money than any man in
England—that I am acquainted with.

Mrs. *THRALE.*

And he has a very pretty talent for poetry. Do you remember his song in "Florizel and Perdita"? "I'd smile with the
simple and feed with the poor."

Dr. *JOHNSON.*

Nay, my dear lady, that will never do. Poor Davy! "Smile
with the simple"—what folly is this! And who would "feed
with the poor" that can help it? No, no, let me smile with
the wise and feed with the rich — as I shall shortly be doing.
Life here, madam, is as near felicity as life may be expected to
be. But where is little Burney? We are neglecting her shame-
fully.

Mrs. *THRALE.*

Over on the sofa yonder in the company of Sir Joshua Reynolds.

Dr. *JOHNSON.*

She could not possibly be in better. He has known her for
many years without in the least suspecting she was a genius;
the little hussy. I must sit by her at dinner.

Mrs. *THRALE.*

So you shall, but will not her head be turned with all this
flattery?

Dr. *JOHNSON.*

Dr. *JOHNSON.*

Why, no, madam, the established wits will keep her in her place. It will be difficult for her to maintain herself in conversation, for observation rather than retort is her forte. She will need all her friends. When one bursts unheralded on the town, the town feels cheated of watching an ascent. [*They approach Miss Burney, who is talking to Sir Joshua Reynolds through his ear trumpet.*]

Miss *BURNEY.*

Yes, sir, I sold the manuscript to Mr. Lowndes for twenty guineas and thought I had done excellently well for myself.

Sir *JOSHUA.*

Twenty guineas! My dear young lady, the book was worth a hundred, but one has to make a beginning. I sat up all night reading it and had to deny myself to some sitters the next day. I shall recommend it to all my friends, and make it unfashionable not to have read it. [*Dr. Johnson comes up.*] We were talking of *Evelina.*

Dr. *JOHNSON.*

The subject is inexhaustible. I am to sit next to Miss Burney at dinner; I shall be very proud.

Sir *JOSHUA.*

We shall have to be very careful or she may put us into her next book: her power of observation is so remarkable — her portraits would be unmistakable.

Dr. *JOHNSON.*

Dr. *JOHNSON*.

She would not dare burlesque her friends.

Miss *MORE*.

[*Joining the party.*] Oh, I 'm sure she would not. Consider, Dr. Johnson, the respect we have for you, it amounts almost to a feeling of awe. Peers obey your nod, and I am told that Duchesses hang upon your words, that your company is more sought than that of any man in London.

Dr. *JOHNSON*.

Stop! madam, stop! Consider what your flattery is worth before you choke me to death with it. [*More kindly.*] You are permitted to say some things behind a man's back that you would not say to his face.

Miss *MORE*.

I heard Bishop Percy say at Chesterfield House that you could by giving a sign make or break a literary reputation.

Dr. *JOHNSON*.

Madam, I take refuge in incredulity.

Miss *MORE*.

I am so sorry that I never saw your play, *Irene;* I have read that it was the finest tragedy of modern times.

Dr. *JOHNSON*.

You have not read that statement in a bound book, madam.

Miss *MORE*.

Miss *MORE*.

It was written by one Pott.

Dr. *JOHNSON*.

Madam, if one Pott says so, Pott lies. [*Walks away as James Boswell comes up.*]

Miss *MORE*.

Mr. Boswell, I understand that you are collecting material to write the life of our revered friend; I trust it may be many years before you do so, but should the time come, you will, I hope, mitigate somewhat the asperities of his disposition.

Mr. *BOSWELL*.

Madam, I shall not cut his claws or make my tiger a cat to please anybody. I may ask Miss Burney here to give me some anecdotes as she sees the great dictionary-maker in *déshabillé*, as it were. I know Dr. Johnson, the lexicographer, the philosopher and moralist, but you know Johnson, the ladies' man—a side that is hidden from me.

Miss *BURNEY*.

And if I do, Mr. Boswell, I shall impart my knowledge to my only confidant—my journal.

Mr. *BOSWELL*.

I am not to be balked of my purpose of making a well-rounded portrait, to which end I shall apply to Mrs. Thrale. [*Addressing himself to that lady.*] Ah, madam, have
you

you not repeatedly heard Dr. Johnson say that if he had no duties, he would spend his life driving briskly in a postchaise with a pretty woman?

Mrs. *THRALE.*

I have never heard Dr. Johnson say any one thing repeatedly, he has too fertile a mind for that; but I have heard him utter the sentiment you refer to, adding, but she should be one who could understand me and add something to the pleasure of conversation.

Mr. *BOSWELL.*

I have upon occasions visited the greenrooms with him and the actresses invariably make much of him; Mrs. Abington positively flirted with him, and we all know how partial he is to Kitty Clive.

Mrs. *THRALE.*

Certainly; I have heard him declare that she was a better romp than ever he saw in nature.

Mr. *BOSWELL.*

And he is not without experience. When we were on our journey to the Hebrides, a lively pretty young woman, hearing that he was come from London, peeped into the room in which we were sitting to have a glimpse of the great lexicographer. Some of her friends dared her to place herself upon his knee, put her arms around his neck and give him a kiss. She took the dare, and what do you think the Doctor said?

Mrs. *THRALE.*

Mrs. *THRALE.*

I hope he corrected the brazen hussy!

Mr. *BOSWELL.*

Not at all, madam. He was quite equal to the occasion. He
said: "Do it again, let us see who gets tired first."

Dr. *GOLDSMITH.*

[*Coming up.*] I am quite at a loss to account for his popularity:
I have observed that women frequently prefer his company
to that of men of much greater physical and at least equal mental attractions. And men sometimes surrender their minds to
his in a most surprising manner. A few moments ago a gentleman said "Doctor" and I, naturally, turned towards him, and
what do you suppose he said?—"No, 't is not you I mean,
Dr. Minor, 't is Dr. Major there." It is enough to make a
man commit suicide. [*Dr. Johnson overhears the last part of the
conversation.*]

Dr. *JOHNSON.*

[*Meditatively.*] Death will overtake us all too soon, no need to
summon him. [*Rousing himself.*] Sir, let the subject alone: you
write well, be satisfied with that and do not seek always to
shine in conversation.

Dr. *GOLDSMITH.*

Oh, Dr. Johnson, that reminds me, I have written a fable
which I wish to submit to you: A school of little fishes, seeing that birds can fly in the air which covers both the land
and

and water alike, while they would die if they were taken from the water, petition Jupiter to change them into birds, —

Dr. *JOHNSON*.

[*Laughing.*] Such writing is very easy.

Dr. *GOLDSMITH*.

Why, sir, it is not as easy as you seem to think; if you were to make little fishes talk, they would talk like whales.

[*Dr.* Johnson, *blowing like a whale, retires.*

Footman announces Mr. Piozzi, *Mrs.* Carter, *Miss* Streatfield. *Enter a distinguished foreign looking gentleman, who bows very low to Mrs. Thrale, a charming old lady in an elaborate cap, and a very beautiful young woman, whose chief accomplishment appears to have been ability to force real tears to run down her cheeks, much to the delight of Henry Thrale.*

Mrs. *THRALE*.

Buon' giorno, Signor [*with a slight bow*]. Mrs. Carter, welcome, how sweet you look! Sophie, [*to Miss Streatfield*] Mr. Thrale has been asking for you; don't fail to humour him if he asks you to weep for him: he seems very ill to me. [*In a low voice.*] I shall be glad when this dinner is over.

Sir *JOSHUA*.

Dr. Johnson, who is that very charming old lady? I should love to paint her.

Dr. *JOHNSON*.

Dr. *JOHNSON.*

That is my dear friend, Mrs. Elizabeth Carter, the translator of Epictetus — and equally good at making a pudding — a very accomplished woman; let me present you. [*Turning to Mrs. Carter.*] Madam, I am pleased to see you; my friend Sir Joshua Reynolds craves the honour of your acquaintance. [*They bow.*] I have told him of your accomplishments, not the least of which is your skill — with a pudding.

Mr. *THRALE.*

[*To Sophie Streatfield.*] You are looking very well to-day; strange that tears which spoil other faces only increase the beauty of yours. [*She takes his offered arm.*]

Mr. *BOSWELL.*

Dr. Johnson, have you met Dr. Franklin of Pennsylvania? He is a most distinguished man.

Dr. *JOHNSON.*

"Distinguished in Pennsylvania!" sir, but what is he in London? I have heard of his endeavour to force his acquaintance upon Mr. Gibbon.

Mr. *BOSWELL.*

Mr. Gibbon is an ugly, disgusting man and poisons our club for me.

Sir *JOSHUA.*

When did he meet Dr. Franklin?

Dr. *JOHNSON.*

Dr. *JOHNSON*.

Why, sir, it appears that Mr. Gibbon and Dr. Franklin, as you call him, were spending a night at the same inn on the road to Paris. Franklin, discovering that Gibbon and he were under the same roof, sent the landlord to say that he would be pleased to pass the evening with him, to which Mr. Gibbon very properly replied that while he esteemed him as a man, yet as an enemy to his King and country he had no wish to make his acquaintance.

Sir *JOSHUA*.

Very well said.

Mr. *BOSWELL*.

But, sir, you appear not to have heard the sequel. Dr. Franklin, in a polite note, replied that when in the course of Mr. Gibbon's writing of the decline and fall of empires he came to write of the decline and fall of the British Empire, he would be happy to furnish him with such material as might otherwise escape his attention.

Dr. *JOHNSON*.

A fly, sir, may sting a noble animal, but it yet remains a fly. I am willing to love all mankind except an American; they are a race of convicts and ought to be thankful for anything we do to them short of hanging.

Miss *MORE*.

Dr. Johnson, I am going to ask if you will oblige me by looking over the pages of a tragedy I am writing. I have not quite finished it yet — I have so many irons in the fire.

Dr. *JOHNSON*.

Dr. *JOHNSON*.

Then, madam, I would urge you to put your tragedy in the fire along with your irons.

Mrs. *THRALE*.

Dr. Johnson, here is a lady, a very particular friend of mine, anxious to make your acquaintance. Mrs. Delaney, I present my good friend Dr. Johnson.

Dr. *JOHNSON*.

I am honoured by your notice, madam.

Mrs. *DELANEY*.

Your Dictionary, sir, has given me so much pleasure — while it changes the subject very often —

Dr. *JOHNSON*.

I confess that it does, madam, have that fault in common with most dictionaries.

Mrs. *DELANEY*.

I observed with pleasure that it has very few naughty words in it, —

Dr. *JOHNSON*.

I hope, madam, that you have not been looking for them.

Mrs. *DELANEY*.

Oh! fie, Dr. Johnson, how can you say such a thing? I did, however, observe that you omitted altogether the word *Ocean*.

Dr. *JOHNSON*.

Dr. *JOHNSON.*

Omit the word *ocean*, madam, impossible! [*Stalking across the room to the Dictionary, which lies upon a table, finding the word, and pointing to it.*] There is the word, madam, but you would look for it in vain if you spell it o-s-h-u-n.

Mr. *BOSWELL.*

I have compared your work with that of the French Academy and I am overjoyed to see in how many respects it excels,—

Dr. *JOHNSON.*

Why, sir, what would you expect from fellows that eat frogs?

Mr. *BOSWELL.*

Did the making of the definitions give you much trouble?

Dr. *JOHNSON.*

Thought rather than trouble. We all know what light is, but it is not easy to tell what it is.

Mrs. *DELANEY.*

But, sir, how came you to define *pastern* as the knee of a horse?

Dr. *JOHNSON.*

Ignorance, madam, pure ignorance. The fact is, a dictionary is like a watch, the worst is better than none and the best cannot be expected to go always right.

Mr. Baretti, *the Italian tutor in the Thrale family, coming up unannounced.*

Ah!

Ah! Baretti, here I am, placed on the defensive by a lady who challenges the definitions in my Dictionary.

Mr. *BARETTI*.

To frivolous censure, sir, no other answer is necessary than that supplied by your own very excellent preface. The Dictionary is a monument of scholarship, and I deeply regret that the Italian language has nothing comparable with it.

Mr. *BOSWELL*.

Dr. Johnson, were you disturbed when the town, having in mind your definition of pension,—"An allowance made to any one without an equivalent; in England it is generally understood to mean pay given to a state hireling for treason to his country,"—criticized you for the acceptance of one?

Dr. *JOHNSON*.

Disturbed at the criticism of the town! Certainly not! I wish my pension had been twice as large that the public could have made twice as much fuss about it. The pension, sir, was given not for anything I was to do, but for what I had already done.

Mr. *THRALE*.

[*In a loud voice.*] I have an announcement to make: Few of my guests know that this company is assembled in honour of Mrs. Thrale's birthday. We shall drink her health at the table, meantime I wish to present her with these flowers. [*Handing her a huge bouquet of roses.*]

Mrs. *THRALE*.

Mrs. *THRALE*.

Oh, sir, you embarrass me; at my time of life, birthdays are
more honoured in the breach than in the observance.

Mr. *BOSWELL*.

I assure you, madam, the years have left no trace; you might
indeed be taken for one of your own daughters.

Mrs. *THRALE*.

You flatter me. And you are at the same time busying yourself with the problem, How old is she? Well, I confess to
[*with a smile*] thirty-five. [*Pouting.*] Nobody sends me verses
nowadays, yet Swift fed Stella with them till she was six and
forty, I remember. Do, Dr. Johnson, make a set, impromptu,
with the rhyme on thirty-five—not more, remember.

Dr. *JOHNSON*.

[*Walking up and down in deep thought, clapping his hands together,
quite unconsciously attracting the attention of all.*] Why, madam, a
request from a lady upon her birthday is in the nature of a
command. Let me see. [*Very slowly, until he gets fairly started.*]

> " *Oft in danger, yet alive,*
> *We are come to thirty-five;*
> *Long may better years arrive,*
> *Better years than thirty-five.*
> *Could philosophers contrive*
> *Life to stop at thirty-five,*
> *Time his hours should never drive*
> *O'er the bounds of thirty-five.*

High

High to soar, and deep to dive,
Nature gives at thirty-five.
Ladies, stock and tend your hive,
Trifle not at thirty-five;
For howe'er we boast and strive,
Life declines from thirty-five.
He that ever hopes to thrive
Must begin at thirty-five;
And all who wisely wish to wive
Must look on Thrale at thirty-five."

[*There is much applause, during which can be heard:*]

Mr. *GARRICK.*

Marvellous.

Mr. *BOSWELL.*

Astonishing.

Mrs. *THRALE.*

Oh, sir, you are a wonderful man!

Dr. *JOHNSON.*

Nay, madam: now you see what it is to come to a dictionary-maker for verses. Do you observe that the rhymes run in alphabetical order exactly?

Mrs. *THRALE.*

Which only increases my amazement.

Mr. *MURPHY.*

Let me shake your hand, sir. You have given us a wonderful example of your readiness, astounding, at your age. What
would

would you not give, sir, to be thirty-five once more yourself?

Dr. *JOHNSON.*

Why, sir, I should be content to be as foolish, almost, as you
are.

Mr. *MURPHY.*

But we are getting on, Dr. Johnson, we are getting on.

Dr. *JOHNSON.*

We are, sir, as you say, getting on, but that is no reason why
we should discourage one another.

Mr. *MURPHY.*

You are a philosopher, sir. I have tried, too, in my time to
be a philosopher, but I don't know how: cheerfulness was
always breaking in.

Mrs. *THRALE.*

Signor Piozzi has been good enough to yield to my persuasions
and will play and sing for us that exquisite "Aria Parlante,"
which is the talk of the town, if we may have a moment's
quiet. [*Conversation ceases. Signor Piozzi takes his place at the
pianoforte and for a few moments plays and sings very agreeably.
When he ceases there is a rush to thank and congratulate him. Dr.
Johnson only seems unimpressed.*]

Mr. *GARRICK.*

Superbly done! [*To Dr. Johnson.*] That piece is very difficult.

Dr. *JOHNSON.*

Dr. *JOHNSON.*

Sir, I would that it had been impossible.

Mr. *BOSWELL.*

Dr. Johnson, we have had good talk. You have tossed and gored several persons. It is a pleasant company.

Dr. *JOHNSON.*

Why, sir, Mr. Thrale gathers about him the best — I will not say the highest — company in London. He is a remarkable man. I honour him; if his mind marks the hours rather than the minutes, it is enough. He does not burden himself with details.

Mr. *BOSWELL.*

He is a gentleman.

Dr. *JOHNSON.*

He is, sir, a new species of gentleman, living, as you see, in vulgar prosperity.

Mr. *BOSWELL.*

His time is, I suppose, largely spent in making money.

Dr. *JOHNSON.*

It is, sir, and there are indeed few ways in which a man can be more innocently employed than in making money.

Mr. *BOSWELL.*

He might devote himself to literature.

Dr. *JOHNSON.*

Dr. *JOHNSON.*

For his amusement, sir: the happiest life is that of a man of business with some literary pursuits for his amusement.

Enter Footman, *who throws open the doors.*

FOOTMAN.

Dinner is on the table.

Dr. *JOHNSON.*

Good! A time comes in a man's life when he is in need of the repairs of the table.

> [*Immediately a procession is formed. Two by two in "tragedy step" they enter the dining-room: Mr. Thrale with Sophie Streatfield on his arm; Mr. Murphy offers his arm to Miss Burney, who accepts it, upon which Dr. Johnson almost knocks over several people in an effort to retrieve Miss Burney, which he at last does, much to Mr. Murphy's chagrin. Mrs. Thrale puts her arm through Mr. Murphy's and leads him in, as the curtains falls.*

[*The curtain remains down one minute to suggest the lapse of one hour; when it is raised the stage is deserted. Almost immediately the doors to the dining-room are thrown open and a number of the guests rush out in great confusion.*]

Mr. *GARRICK.*

Mr. Thrale will recover: he has had these attacks before.

Mr. *MURPHY.*

Mr. *MURPHY.*

That is the trouble; he has been repeatedly warned by his physician against overeating. I observed that he had become very flushed just before he fell forward.

Miss *STREATFIELD.*

Is he dead?

Mr. *GARRICK.*

No, but the attack is a severe one. He must be bled.

Mrs. *THRALE.*

Oh, sir, let no time be lost; these attacks come with increasing frequency.

Dr. *JOHNSON.*

[*Taking control of the situation.*]

[*To a Servant.*] Send a man at once on horseback to Dr. Brocklesby and tell him a valuable life is at stake. Meanwhile Mr. Thrale must be got to his bed. Dr. Goldsmith will give us the benefit of his skill. He has not, I hope, forgotten the use of a lancet.

[*Curtain falls as Henry Thrale is seen quite unconscious in a large chair carried by two servants.*

Act III.

Characters in Act III.

Dr. *JOHNSON*.
SERVANT.
Mrs. *THRALE*.
Mr. *BOSWELL*.
Mr. *BARCLAY*.
Mr. *PERKINS*.
Miss *BURNEY*.
Miss *THRALE*.

ACT III.

The morning room at Streatham. A large, bright, comfortable apartment with a fireplace in which a wood fire is burning brightly; with doors to right and left. Between the large casement windows, which open to the floor, are open shelves filled with books. On the walls are a number of fine mezzotint portraits of the famous authors, statesmen, and actors of the period. There are several large writing-tables, with pens, ink, and paper at hand. Easy chairs are conveniently placed on either side of the fireplace and at the windows. The room is suggestive of what might be called scholarly comfort. On the hearthrug a large dog is seen, asleep, otherwise the room is deserted. The time is about noon. More than a year has passed since the last act.

Dr. JOHNSON *enters and looks around.*

Dr. *JOHNSON.*

MADAM, are you here? [*To himself.*] I love not to come down to vacuity. [*Walking towards the fireplace and seeing the dog.*] Presto, you are, if possible, a lazier dog than I am. [*Going to the bell pull and giving it a tug. After a moment a* SERVANT *appears.*] Have you seen Mrs. Thrale this morning?

SERVANT.

Yes, sir, Mrs. Thrale had breakfast some time ago with Miss Burney. They are, I think, walking in the grounds. Shall I go fetch them, sir?

Dr. *JOHNSON.*

Dr. *JOHNSON.*

Yes, do,—no, wait a minute. I shall not send for her. No, bring me my breakfast.

SERVANT.

Yes, sir, will you be 'aving some cold chicken and 'am, sir?

Dr. *JOHNSON.*

Yes, whatever there is, in some quantity; I am hungry this morning.

SERVANT.

Will you look at the paper, sir?

Dr. *JOHNSON.*

No,—yes, bring it to me.   [SERVANT *leaves the room.* [*Speaking to himself.*] One-half that one reads in the papers is not true; the other half is not important. [*Rather irritably.*] Surely Mrs. Thrale knows that I do not like to eat alone. [*Enter* SERVANT *with newspaper and large tray of breakfast sundries, which he places on the table before Dr. Johnson, who at once begins eating. After a few moments he opens paper and presently begins to read aloud.*] "Subscribers are beginning to wonder whether they will ever receive the long-promised edition of Shakespeare from the hands of Dr. Johnson. If it is not soon delivered in the ordinary way, a Cæsarian operation may become necessary." What's this? [*Continuing to read.*]

> " *He for subscribers baits his hook*
> *And takes your cash, but where's the book?*

No

No matter where : wise fear, you know,
Forbids the robbing of a foe;
But what, to serve our private ends,
Forbids the cheating of our friends?"

That's Churchill, the scoundrel! This must not be permitted. I have, unluckily, lost the list of my subscribers and spent the money, but by labour the damage can be repaired. [*After a pause.*] This attack will have only temporary currency. I must set about this work to-morrow. "To-morrow, and to-morrow, and to-morrow." Why is not my lady here to pour out my tea? [*After a pause.*] He who dislikes his own company cannot be certain that it will be enjoyed by others. Ah! here she is.

Enter Mrs. THRALE, *charmingly dressed in a white frock with black ribbons, carrying a great basket of roses in her arms; she proceeds to arrange these in vases around the room.*

Dear madam, I have been longing for you, I am indeed lonely when you are absent.

Mrs. *THRALE.*

Good morning, my dear Dr. Johnson. I cannot always be here; I have, as you know, many domestic duties. Is not Fanny about? She should have poured your tea.

Dr. *JOHNSON.*

I have seen no one but the servant, madam, and he is as sleepy as a dormouse. Fanny is probably engaged upon her book, an example I would do well to follow. Have you seen
this

this attack on me in the paper? [*Handing Mrs. Thrale the paper.*]

Mrs. *THRALE.*

[*Glancing at it.*] Yes, I saw it; what shall you do about it?

Dr. *JOHNSON.*

Ignore it, madam. I would rather be attacked than unnoticed. An attack upon an author does him a service. A man who says my book is bad is less my enemy than he who lets it die in silence.

Mrs. *THRALE.*

A man's fame is different from a woman's.

Dr. *JOHNSON.*

It is, madam. A man's fame is a shuttlecock; if it be struck only at one end of the room it falls to the ground. Instead of being angry at those who write against me, I should smile to think that they are unintentionally keeping me before the public.

Enter RATTLE.

Mrs. *THRALE.*

What is it, Rattle?

RATTLE.

Miss Esther, madam, has a sore throat, madam, she wishes you would come to her.

Mrs. *THRALE.*

Those children of mine are always catching something. Tell her I shall be with her directly.

RATTLE.

RATTLE.

Yes, madam.   [*Goes out.*

Mrs. *THRALE.*

You must, sir, finish your Shakespeare. [*Goes to the mantel-piece and takes some papers therefrom.*] I find your notes all over the house. [*Reading.*] "Notes are often necessary, but they are necessary evils. Let him that is as yet unacquainted with the powers of Shakespeare, and who desires to feel the highest pleasure that the drama can give, read every play from the first scene to the last, with utter negligence of all his commentators." Excellent advice, sir, but it is a pity that it should be lost upon my mantelpiece. It should be in a book, sir, a bound book. And now you must excuse me, I must go to Queenie.   [*Goes out.*

Dr. *JOHNSON.*

[*To himself.*] I shall send for Fanny. She shall keep me company. [*He sits alone for a moment and then crosses the room to the bell pull.*]

Enter SERVANT.

SERVANT.

As I came through the 'all, sir, I 'eard a gentleman hasking for you, sir. I think it is Mr. Boswell, sir.

Dr. *JOHNSON.*

Show him in at once. [*To himself, cheerfully.*] It is always pleasant to see Jamie.

Mr. BOSWELL.

Mr. Boswell *enters.*

Ah, Bozzy, I am glad to see you. I hope I see you well. Just come from Scotland? [*They shake hands cordially.*]

Mr. *BOSWELL.*

Yes, sir, I arrived last evening and put up for the night at the Saracen's Head. You know the place, sir.

Dr. *JOHNSON.*

Yes, sir, on Snow Hill, and a most excellent inn it is; there is no private house in which people can enjoy themselves so well as at a capital inn. I sometimes think a tavern chair is the throne of human felicity.

Mr. *BOSWELL.*

But, sir, as I hope to remain in London for some time, I desired a more convenient location and have taken lodgings in Great Queen Street, off Lincoln's Inn Fields. And how are my friends Mrs. Williams, Levett, and the rest of your household?

Dr. *JOHNSON.*

Sir, we have tolerable concord at home but no love. Williams hates everybody. Levett hates Desmoulins and does not love Williams. Desmoulins hates them both. Poll loves none of them.

Mr. *BOSWELL.*

I cannot understand, sir, how you can surround yourself with such necessitous and undeserving people.

Dr. *JOHNSON.*

Dr. *JOHNSON.*

If I did not assist them, no one else would, and they must
be lost for want.

Mr. *BOSWELL.*

And your work, sir. How have you been employing your
time? Does your Shakespeare go forward?

Dr. *JOHNSON.*

Sir, for years I beat the track of the alphabet with sluggish
resolution. Since I have spent so much of my time here, in
the broad sunshine of life, I have lived a life of total idleness
and the pride of literature. But I must amend my ways. And
how did you leave your lady?

Mr. *BOSWELL.*

Not as well as might be; she has indeed been threatened with
a consumption, but it is now mending. She has sent you a
pot of marmalade of her own making which I shall deliver
at your lodgings in Bolt Court.

Dr. *JOHNSON.*

That is kind, particularly as she does not love me. Is it a
peace offering? I have not forgotten her remark: "I have seen
many a bear led by a man, but never before a man led by a
bear." One does not love to be called a bear.

Mr. *BOSWELL.*

Why, sir, my wife thinks doubtless you have too great an in-
fluence over her husband, which is perhaps not unnatural to

a

a female mind, but at heart she reveres you almost as much as I do.

Dr. *JOHNSON*.

I wish I could think so.

Mr. *BOSWELL*.

It is delightful, sir, to be in London again.

Dr. *JOHNSON*.

Why, sir, you will find no man at all intellectual who does not delight in London. When a man is tired of London he is tired of life, for there is in London all that life can afford. But, sir, I never knew any one with such a gust for the town as you have.

Mr. *BOSWELL*.

The streets, sir, are so animated, I love the life in the taverns, the eating, — yes, sir, and the drinking, — and the play. They are, I hear, giving an excellent performance of "The Beggar's Opera" at Drury Lane.

Dr. *JOHNSON*.

So I understand, but I do not now go much to the play; my eyesight is failing, and my hearing, as you know, has long been defective.

Mr. *BOSWELL*.

Call remembrance to your aid, sir: you have not forgotten, I am sure, the charms of Lavinia Fenton. Was she not a delightful Polly?

Dr. *JOHNSON*.

Dr. *JOHNSON*.

She was indeed, sir, in spite of the painful and ridiculous
lines:

> " *For on the rope that hangs my Dear*
> *Depends poor Polly's life.*"

You doubtless best remember the lines sung by Macheath:

> " *How happy could I be with either*
> *Were t'other dear charmer away.*"

Mr. *BOSWELL*.

Why yes, sir, it is, I believe, an entirely masculine sentiment.

Dr. *JOHNSON*.

Sir, I believe it is.

Mr. *BOSWELL*.

But, Miss Fenton: I have heard that she became the mistress of the Duke of Bolton and that he has married her. I
hope he may be happy.

Dr. *JOHNSON*.

Sir, love and marriage are different states. He wanted to
gratify his passion, the wench wanted a husband and a title,
both are suited. The match was not, I should say, made in
Heaven.

Mr. *BOSWELL*.

Pray, sir, do you not suppose that there are fifty women in
the world with any one of whom a man may be as happy as
with any one woman in particular?

Dr. *JOHNSON*.

Dr. *JOHNSON.*

Aye, sir, fifty thousand.

Mr. *BOSWELL.*

Then, sir, you are not of the opinion of those who imagine that certain men and certain women are made for each other, and that they cannot be happy if they miss their counterparts.

Dr. *JOHNSON.*

To be sure not, sir. I believe that marriages would in general be as happy, and often more so, if they were all made by the Lord Chancellor upon a due consideration of the characters and circumstances, without the parties having any choice in the matter.

Mr. *BOSWELL.*

In your judgment, Dr. Johnson, should a man invariably marry?

Dr. *JOHNSON.*

Why, sir, I would advise no man to marry who is not likely to propagate understanding. Marriage is much more necessary for a man than for a woman, for he is much less able to supply himself with domestic comforts.

Mr. *BOSWELL.*

It would appear so. Quite recently, sir, a friend who had been notoriously unhappy with his wife, upon her death immediately married again.

Dr. *JOHNSON.*

Dr. *JOHNSON.*

That, sir, might be called the triumph of hope over experience.

Mr. *BOSWELL.*

Dr. Johnson, have you ever considered the possibility of a second marriage?

Dr. *JOHNSON.*

Why yes, sir, frequently; indeed, I may say that I have been thinking of it this very morning.

Mr. *BOSWELL.*

You amaze me, sir!

Dr. *JOHNSON.*

And why, sir? I was very happy with Mrs. Johnson; her birthday, our wedding day, and the day of her death, have been generally kept by me with solemn observation. By taking a second wife I pay the highest possible compliment to my first. Marriage would enable me to enjoy the continuance of domestic comfort to which I have long been accustomed. Marriage is the best state for man in general, and every man is a worse man in proportion as he is unfit for it.

Mr. *BOSWELL.*

But, sir, you are, it would seem, very comfortably settled here.

Dr. *JOHNSON.*

Why, in some sort, I am; but since the death of Henry Thrale there is something lacking in this establishment. The
household

household lacks a head, as does the business; indeed, it is Mrs. Thrale's wish that the brewery be disposed of. As one of the executors of Thrale's will, I stood out against it, but I know not why I should be concerned: there is no male heir to succeed to the business, and the estate could be the more easily cared for if it were sold, and the proceeds invested in the funds. Indeed, a knot of rich Quakers are to call this very morning to discuss the matter.

Mr. BOSWELL.

In which case I should be going, but I would be glad to say a word of greeting to Mrs. Thrale before I take my departure.

Dr. JOHNSON.

I will send for the lady, if you will be good enough to ring. [*Boswell goes to the bell pull*.] Thank you. How did you leave my Lord of Auchinleck, your father? You keep on good terms with him, I hope.

Mr. BOSWELL.

Passably, sir. We differ over money matters: he recently paid bills for me to the sum of a thousand pounds, but I am still in some distress over a number of small debts.

Dr. JOHNSON.

Small debts are like small shot: they are rattling on every side and can scarcely be escaped without a wound; great debts are like cannon, of loud noise but little danger.

Mr. BOSWELL.

Just my experience, sir. Your readiness never ceases to amaze
me:

me: you instantly put into words thoughts which we ordinary mortals but clumsily revolve in our minds.

Dr. *JOHNSON.*

Why, sir, in conversation I admit to a certain verbal facility. But Mrs. Thrale will wish me to extend the hospitality of this house: will you have chocolate or join me in a cup of tea?

Mr. *BOSWELL.*

Thank you, sir, but I breakfasted not much over an hour ago, you will excuse me,—

Dr. *JOHNSON.*

And my other friends in Edinburgh, how did you leave them?

Mr. *BOSWELL.*

Very well, sir; Lord Monboddo desired me very particularly to present his compliments to you.

Dr. *JOHNSON.*

He still insists that mankind is descended from monkeys. [*Laughing.*] And is still searching for his own tail, I suppose? If he wishes to own a monkey for his ancestor, I know not why I should dispute his claim.

Enter Servant.

Will you say to my lady that Mr. James Boswell has just arrived from Scotland and would pay his respects to her if she is disengaged?

SERVANT.

SERVANT.

Yes, sir.   [*Goes out.*

Mr. *BOSWELL.*

I often think, sir, of our tour to the Hebrides, I hope the remembrance of it gives you as much pleasure as it does me.

Dr. *JOHNSON.*

Why, sir, I do not know how much pleasure you derive from the remembrance, but it was the most pleasant frolic I ever had, and I would not for five hundred pounds forego the recollection of it. If you and I live to be old men, we shall take great delight in talking over our experiences.

Mr. *BOSWELL.*

Why should we wait to be old to enjoy that pleasure? Do you remember, sir, our experiences on the vessel going to Mull and how seasick you were?

Dr. *JOHNSON.*

I do not, indeed, look back upon that particular experience with any great amount of pleasure.

Mr. *BOSWELL.*

And yet, sir, the sailors did not seem to heed the storm.

Dr. *JOHNSON.*

A storm makes a sailor but little more miserable than he is already. No man will be a sailor who has contrivance enough to get himself into a jail, for being in a ship is like being in a jail, with the added chance of being drowned.

Mr. *BOSWELL.*

Mr. *BOSWELL.*

And what has become of your great brown-cloth coat with the side pockets, each of which might almost have held a volume of your Dictionary?

Dr. *JOHNSON.*

Why, sir, I brought that safely home with me. And my great oak stick that I carried all the way from London, and which I was going to present to some museum, which disappeared so unaccountably: you never heard of it again, I suppose?

Mr. *BOSWELL.*

No, sir, as you said at the time, "Consider the value of such a piece of timber in Mull; it was not to be expected that the man who found it would part with it."

Dr. *JOHNSON.*

Why no, sir, being a Scotchman; you are to consider that there is very little soil in Scotland and very few trees, it indeed chiefly consists of stone and water.

Mr. *BOSWELL.*

It does, sir, but you will admit that Scotland has a great many noble, wild prospects.

Dr. *JOHNSON.*

Sir, it has, and so has Norway; and Lapland is remarkable for its prodigious, noble, wild prospects. But, sir, let me tell you that the noblest prospect which a Scotchman ever sees is the high road that leads him to England.

Mr. *BOSWELL.*

Mr. *BOSWELL.*

Dr. Johnson, you seem to forget that God made Scotland.

Dr. *JOHNSON.*

I remember, sir, that he made it for Scotchmen.

Mr. *BOSWELL.*

We are a fine, sturdy race, sir.

Dr. *JOHNSON.*

Why yes, sir, I believe you are. Goldsmith says somewhere that man is the only animal that has reached a natural size in your country.

Mr. *BOSWELL.*

Ah, sir, since we last met we have experienced a great loss: Goldsmith has been taken from us.

Dr. *JOHNSON.*

Do not speak of it, sir; I cannot think of it with tranquillity.

Mr. *BOSWELL.*

Was he buried in the Abbey, sir?

Dr. *JOHNSON.*

No, sir, in the Temple. He was greatly in debt at the time of his death and it was thought that there might have been a scandal. He was buried at night in ground just north of the Temple Church: it was very solemn.

Mr. *BOSWELL.*

Mr. *BOSWELL.*

I have heard that he was careless in money matters.

Dr. *JOHNSON.*

He was, sir, but let not his frailties be remembered, he was
a very great man: he left scarcely any style of writing un-
touched, and touched nothing that he did not adorn.

Mr. *BOSWELL.*

And Garrick, sir, his death is a great loss.

Dr. *JOHNSON.*

I never think of Garrick but the tears come into my eyes.
Garrick's death eclipsed the gaiety of nations and impover-
ished the public stock of harmless pleasure. Why, sir, I would
not hear of the election of his successor in our Club until
he had been dead a year: I insisted that we undergo a year's
widowhood.

Mr. *BOSWELL.*

I knew that he was one of your oldest friends.

Dr. *JOHNSON.*

We came to London together, penniless; that is to say, I
had tuppence in my pocket and he had three ha'pence in his.

Mr. *BOSWELL.*

I have heard that he died a very rich man.

Dr. *JOHNSON.*

Dr. *JOHNSON.*

Sir, no actor has ever enjoyed the public esteem so much as Garrick. His profession made him rich, and he made his profession respectable.

Mr. *BOSWELL.*

He rests, I believe, in the Abbey?

Dr. *JOHNSON.*

Yes, sir, and properly, at the foot of Shakespeare's monument.

Mr. *BOSWELL.*

I shall place a wreath upon his grave;

"a merrier man,
Within the limit of becoming mirth,
I never spent an hour's talk withal."

Dr. *JOHNSON.*

And I will go with you, and afterwards we will call upon his lady in the Adelphi.

Enter Mrs. THRALE.

Mrs. *THRALE.*

Mr. Boswell, I hope I see you well. [*They shake hands.*]

Mr. *BOSWELL.*

Madam, your most obedient.

Mrs. *THRALE.*

Mrs. *THRALE.*

Shall you stay long with us? I have heard you say that no lover ever longed for his mistress with greater ardour than you for London.

Mr. *BOSWELL.*

Why, madam, that is so: it is my hope to spend several months in town. It has been several years since I was last in London, during which time there have been many and sad changes.

Mrs. *THRALE.*

Yes, and more are impending. Since Mr. Thrale's death and the marriage of several of my daughters, Streatham has become a burden. Neither education nor inclination fits me for the management of a great business; of all things, I loathe a brewery with its mysterious adulterations.

Dr. *JOHNSON.*

Well, madam, we hope soon to relieve you of that burden.

Mrs. *THRALE.*

Then I think I shall retire to Brighthelmstone for a season.

Dr. *JOHNSON.*

Surely, madam, you would not think of giving up Streatham. Think of the many happy years you have spent here surrounded by such comforts and elegancies as are within the reach of few.

Mrs. *THRALE.*

Mrs. *THRALE*.

My life here may not have been as happy as you think. Mr. Thrale, my late lord and master, was not invariably kind. I married not so much to please myself as to please my family.

Mr. *BOSWELL*.

It may be that you will again think of marriage. Dr. Johnson and I have just been speaking of second marriages and are agreed that they need no defense. There is, I think, nothing more beautiful than a marriage of inclination on both sides.

Enter SERVANT.

SERVANT.

Mr. Barclay and Mr. Perkins are in the drawing-room.

Mr. *BOSWELL*.

[*Rising to go.*] Madam, I kiss your hand. Dr. Johnson, I hope to meet you at the Club on Wednesday. I bid you good morning.   [*Goes out.*

Mrs. *THRALE*.

[*To Servant.*] Mr. Boswell's hat and coat. Ask the gentlemen to join us here.

Dr. *JOHNSON*.

Madam, I have heard your plans with great displeasure. Think well before you leave Streatham, with which you have for so long been identified.

Enter

Enter Mr. BARCLAY *and Mr.* PERKINS.

Mr. *BARCLAY*.

Mrs. Thrale, your servant; Dr. Johnson, yours. We have come in the matter of the brewery. Mr. Perkins and I have caused a very careful inventory of the property to be made, which in essentials agrees with the one you yourself gave us. We have had a number of conferences with our friends in the city, and in all the circumstances feel justified in offering you the princely sum of one hundred and twenty-five thousand pounds for the property.

Dr. *JOHNSON*.

I would decline it, madam. We are not here to sell a parcel of boilers and vats, but the potentiality of growing rich beyond the dreams of avarice.

Mrs. *THRALE*.

I am, sir, of the opinion that we should hold out for one hundred and fifty. With care the property can be enormously developed. Mr. Thrale by his — I regret to say — folly, several times placed it in jeopardy. A saving of only sixpence in a barrel would mean a capital sum at the end of the year, and such economies can, I am sure, be readily effected.

Mr. *PERKINS*.

You forget, madam, that I am entirely familiar with the business and know better than you can possibly do its value to a penny.

Mrs. *THRALE*.

Mrs. *THRALE*.

No, it is because you know the value of the business that I ask for one hundred and fifty thousand. I would not have my daughters say that I am unmindful of their interest.

Mr. *BARCLAY*.

One hundred and twenty-five, madam.

Dr. *JOHNSON*.

Let the subject go over until after we have eaten. A good dinner lubricates business. Shall we stroll through the grounds? The brewery has enabled us to live in some state here for many years. Let me show you the glass houses.

They go out and the curtain falls to suggest the passing of a few hours. When it rises again Miss Burney *is seen reading in a great chair; after a moment she puts down the book.*

Miss *BURNEY*.

[*To herself.*] Excitement is running high in this house, and no wonder. It is not every day that negotiations for the sale of a great business are carried on right under one's very nose. I smell malt and hops now,—

Enter Miss Thrale.

Miss *THRALE*.

Oh, my dear Fanny, have you seen mamma or Dr. Johnson? I wonder where they are? What can be detaining them?

Miss *BURNEY*.

FANNY BURNEY

Miss *BURNEY.*

Transactions of magnitude are not concluded in a minute.

Miss *THRALE.*

I saw from my window a gentleman arrive on horseback. Do you know who he was?

Miss *BURNEY.*

Not his name. He was here for a moment, but was not presented. After he had gone I asked Dr. Johnson who he was, and he said that while he was loath to speak ill of a man behind his back, he believed he was an attorney. Mr. Barclay sent for him.

Miss *THRALE.*

Some time ago the party were walking in the shrubbery, and mamma left them and came to me and said one way or the other the affair will soon be concluded. If all goes well she will wave to me a white pocket handkerchief. [*She goes to a long window, opens it, and looks out.*] I see no one—yes, behind that tree, Dr. Johnson and mamma; where are the others? Can they have gone? Oh, Fanny, come, look! Mamma! she sees me, she waves her handkerchief. The brewery is sold! Now we are no longer in trade and I am an heiress.

[*She goes out at the window, leaving Fanny alone.*

Presently the FOOTMAN *comes in with a large tea tray which he places on the table, as Dr.* JOHNSON, *with several papers in his hand, and Mrs.* THRALE *enter. Mrs. Thrale pours tea.*

Dr. *JOHNSON.*

Dr. *JOHNSON*.

Madam, I congratulate you upon the happy termination of this affair. It only remains for you to add your signature to this agreement. You will sign just above my name. [*Mrs. Thrale signs.*]

Mrs. *THRALE*.

How wonderful it all is! [*Stops pouring tea.*]

Miss *BURNEY*.

I think I shall go in search of Queenie.   [*Leaves.*

Mrs. *THRALE*.

If an angel from heaven had told me thirty years ago that the man I knew by the name of Dictionary Johnson would one day become partner with me in a great trade, and that we should jointly or separately sign notes, drafts, etc., for three or four thousand pounds of a morning and finally dispose of the business for one hundred and fifty thousand pounds, how unlikely it would have seemed ever to happen.

Dr. *JOHNSON*.

Unlikely is not the word, madam. It would have seemed incredible; neither of us was then being worth a groat, and both as far removed from commerce as birth, literature, and inclination could get us.

Mrs. *THRALE*.

I have been accused of being only Mr. Thrale's sleeping partner: what nonsense! However, it is all over now; my three

days

days a week at the counting-house are a thing of the past. Farewell to the brewhouse and to the Borough! Adieu to trade and tradesmen! I have purchased restoration to my original rank in life. I shall retire to Bath and repose my purse.

Dr. *JOHNSON*.
Retire to Bath, madam! Repose your purse! What nonsense is this? Your purse will be equal to the demands made upon it. We live here in comfort, if not in luxury. What more could any woman want?

Mrs. *THRALE*.
She might want a husband.

Dr. *JOHNSON*.
A husband! God forgive you, madam, if I have heard aright.

Mrs. *THRALE*.
Some time since I determined to tell you when I could. Why should I not marry? My children are of age and are independent, as indeed I also am. I love and am loved: if I have concealed the fact from you, it was only to save both of us needless suffering. Speak kindly to me. You make me feel that I am acting without a parent's consent—

Dr. *JOHNSON*.
A parent! I had dared to hope, madam, that your feeling for me was—such—

Mrs. *THRALE*.

Mrs. *THRALE.*

Stop, sir! Dr. Johnson, for many years I have devoted my-self to your service, have been at your beck and call; your comfort was my first, almost my only consideration, but the time has come for me to think of myself. I married once to please my family, I shall shortly marry to please myself, — and one other.

Dr. *JOHNSON.*

You stun me, madam; may I inquire,—

Mrs. *THRALE.*

Certainly, all the world must soon know it: Signor Piozzi.

Dr. *JOHNSON.*

Piozzi! Madam, a foreigner and a fiddler! Impossible!

Mrs. *THRALE.*

Why, sir, it was you who first taught me to respect Mr. Piozzi. I remember well when I met him at an evening party at Dr. Burney's. He was asked to play; I misbehaved, and you reproved me, saying, "Why, madam, because you have no ear for music, do you destroy the performance of a gifted musician?"

Dr. *JOHNSON.*

I may have taught you to respect him, but that is no reason why you should love him. Indeed, I think you cannot be so lost to shame as to abandon yourself, your children, your religion, and your country, for an Italian music master.

Mrs. *THRALE.*

Mrs. *THRALE.*

Wherein is the shame? He loves me and I love him. Know you a better basis for marriage than love?

Dr. *JOHNSON.*

Love! madam. You bewilder me! Are you so lost in self-respect as to throw yourself into the arms of an adventurer? I, who have loved you, esteemed you, reverenced you; I, who for years have thought of you as the first of woman-kind, entreat you to consider before you disgrace yourself.

Mrs. *THRALE.*

Sir, how dare you? In what way would I disgrace myself by marrying Signor Piozzi? His birth is not meaner than that of my first husband, his sentiments are not meaner, his pro-fession is not meaner, and his superiority in that profession is acknowledged by all the world. Is it want of fortune, then, which is ignominious? The character of the man I have chosen has no other claim to such an epithet.

Dr. *JOHNSON.*

His religion?

Mrs. *THRALE.*

The religion to which he is an adherent will, I hope, teach him to forgive insults he has not deserved; mine, I hope, will enable me to bear yours with dignity and patience. The suggestion that I have forfeited my fame is the greatest insult I have yet received. My fame is as unsullied as snow, or I

should

should think it unworthy of him who must henceforth protect it.

Enter Miss THRALE *and Miss* BURNEY.

Miss *THRALE.*

I hear high words. What is the cause?

Dr. *JOHNSON.*

Queenie, your mother has just declared her passion for Piozzi.

Miss *THRALE.*

For Piozzi! Good God! [*Turning to Dr. Johnson.*] Can you not restrain her?

Dr. *JOHNSON.*

I fear, indeed, that she has lost all sense of shame.

Miss *BURNEY.*

Oh, Mrs. Thrale, let me entreat you!

Miss *THRALE.*

I thought I detected her partiality for the music master but hesitated to speak: we are not the best of friends,—

Dr. *JOHNSON.*

If, madam, the last act is yet to do,—

Mrs. *THRALE.*

This is too much. I must ask you, sir, to leave this house and at once.

Dr. *JOHNSON.*

MR. PIOZZI

From a Drawing by George Dance

Dr. *JOHNSON.*

I shall at once obey you, madam. I cannot remain under the roof of one who would indulge herself in such an amour.

Miss *THRALE.*

Can it be that she is my mother?

Mrs. *THRALE.*

[*In tears.*] How can you speak to me so! I have done nothing to deserve this. My child turns against me! Fanny, do you speak to me one word of comfort.

Miss *BURNEY.*

Not I, madam. I blush to be present at such a scene. [*Turning to Miss Thrale.*] My dear, I think we owe it to our characters to leave this house.   [*They go out.*

Dr. *JOHNSON.*

Oh, madam, forgive me. I spoke in haste and in passion. Whatever you have done, however I may lament it, I pray God for your forgiveness: I pray that He may grant you every blessing, that you may be happy now and hereafter. And I ask you to forgive me; I am ready to do what I can to contribute to your happiness in return for that kindness which has soothed twenty years of a life radically wretched.

Mrs. *THRALE.*

That is spoken like my old friend. Only the fear of your disapprobation has given me anxious moments. It would be a
                                                            great

great grief to me to quit England had we unkind feelings
toward each other.

Dr. JOHNSON.

Quit England! Oh, my dear lady, prevail upon Mr. Piozzi
to remain here; you may live here with more dignity than in
Italy and with greater security. Your rank will be higher,
and your fortune more under your own eye. Do not let Mr.
Piozzi or anybody else put me quite out of your head. God's
blessing be upon you, madam, you have always been very
dear to me.   [*Mrs.* THRALE *bows low and goes out.*
[*Dr. Johnson throws himself in a chair, overcome with emotion; pres-*
ently he says:] I shall lose myself in London; in London a man
is always near his burrow. [*Raises his hands in prayer.*] To Thy
Fatherly protection, O Lord, I commend all the members of
this dear family!

Act IV.

Characters in Act IV.

Dr. *JOHNSON.*

FRANK.

Mrs. *DESMOULINS.*

Mr. *HOOLE.*

MARY WOLLSTONECRAFT.

Sir *JOSHUA REYNOLDS.*

Mrs. *SIDDONS.*

Dr. *BROCKLESBY.*

Mr. *WINDHAM.*

Miss *BURNEY.*

Mr. *BURKE.*

YOUNG GIRL.

ACT IV.

A large room in an old house in Bolt Court just off Fleet Street. A door to the right opens into a small passage; door to the left, into a bedroom. Two windows look upon the court. The dark red curtains are drawn. There are several bookcases filled with old books in some confusion. There is also a large table not far from one of the windows on which are two lighted candles, for it is night. A large armchair stands close to the table. An old sofa is in one corner. There are a few unimportant prints on the walls. A fire burns fitfully in a small grate. The time is December 13, 1784. The weather is damp and cold. The room is deserted. Presently Dr. JOHNSON in a long dark dressing-gown, looking very ill, enters, leaning on the arm of his coloured servant, FRANK, followed by Mrs. DESMOULINS. They help him to the large chair, propping him up with pillows.

Mrs. *DESMOULINS.*

ARE you feeling any easier, sir?

Dr. *JOHNSON.*

I fear my days of ease are over, but I should not complain: he that would live to be old has God to thank for the infirmities of age. I may possibly live, at least breathe, three days, perhaps three weeks, but I find myself gradually growing weaker.

FRANK.

Can I do anything for you, sir?

Dr. *JOHNSON.*

Dr. *JOHNSON.*

The Reverend Mr. Hoole promised to come and read the Bible to me; should he come this evening, as I hope he may, admit him promptly.

FRANK.

Yes, sir. I hear steps in the passage. [*Goes to the door, opens it.*]

Mr. HOOLE *enters.*

Mr. *HOOLE.*

My dear friend, I came to redeem my promise. How are you this evening?

Dr. *JOHNSON.*

Do not ask, sir; I am very ill. What is the weather? It has, I think, no effect upon the human frame, but it may powerfully affect one's spirits.

Mr. *HOOLE.*

It is a cold, raw night.

Dr. *JOHNSON.*

I thought so; it is good of you to come to me.

Mr. *HOOLE.*

Not at all. I came to read to you. What shall I read? The prayers for the sick, —

Dr. *JOHNSON.*

No, sir, no. I can pray for myself. Read one of the psalms, —the twenty-third.

Mr. *HOOLE.*

Mr. HOOLE.

[*Takes a Bible from the table, opens it, and begins to read in a low voice.*] "The Lord is my shepherd; I shall not want. He maketh me to lie down in green pastures: he leadeth me beside the still waters. He restoreth my soul:—"

Dr. JOHNSON.

Louder, my dear sir, louder, I entreat you, or you read in vain.

Mr. HOOLE.

"Yea, though I walk through the valley of the shadow of death, I will fear no evil: for thou art with me;—"

Dr. JOHNSON.

I have often wondered when I came to die whether I would wish a friend with me or have it out with God, alone. [*After a pause.*] I have been peevish, sir, you must forgive me; when you are as old and sick as I am perhaps you may be peevish, too.

Mr. HOOLE.

Do not mention it, I beg of you. You are, it seems, a little better.

Dr. JOHNSON.

I think I am. I would give one of these legs for a year more of life, I mean of comfortable life, not such as that I now suffer.

A young lady, MARY WOLLSTONECRAFT, *enters quietly, and addresses Mrs. Desmoulins.*

Mrs. DESMOULINS.

Mrs. *DESMOULINS.*

Miss Wollstonecraft to sit with you, sir. [*She comes forward; Dr. Johnson greets her.*]

Dr. *JOHNSON.*

You have not forgotten me, I see. It is good of you to come. Come sit by me. [*She sits.*]

Miss *WOLLSTONECRAFT.*

I am glad to come. How are you, sir?

Dr. *JOHNSON.*

Very ill, indeed, even with you by my side; think how ill I should be were you at a distance.

Miss *WOLLSTONECRAFT.*

I wish I had something to bring you but I am very poor; a silver teapot is all I own in the world. I have nothing.

Dr. *JOHNSON.*

Don't say so, my dear. You have my heart; I hope you don't call that nothing. Are you still concerning yourself with the wrongs of women?

Miss *WOLLSTONECRAFT.*

Yes, sir, and shall continue to do so, so long as the law discriminates against us.

Dr. *JOHNSON.*

[*With a flash of his old controversial self returning.*] My dear,
Nature

Nature has given women so much power that the law, very wisely, gives them very little.

Miss *WOLLSTONECRAFT.*

But, sir, laws were made by men and imposed upon women. Is that fair?

Dr. *JOHNSON.*

The law is the last result of human wisdom acting upon human experience for the benefit of mankind.

Mr. *HOOLE.*

I must not become involved in this discussion. I am going, sir, and shall meet Dr. Gibbons; have you any message for him?

Dr. *JOHNSON.*

Tell Dr. Gibbons I should be glad to see him. If he'll call on me and dawdle over a cup of tea, I shall take it kind. [*They shake hands.*]

[*Mr.* HOOLE *goes out accompanied by* FRANK.

Miss *WOLLSTONECRAFT.*

I cannot debate with you, sir. I love you, sir, and wish I could revere your opinions as I do you.

Dr. *JOHNSON.*

I used to debate mightily for the sport of it, but it fatigues me now. I am a sick old man.

Miss *WOLLSTONECRAFT.*

Miss *WOLLSTONECRAFT*.

I should not have troubled you, sir, with my opinions. I shall not when I come again. May I come again?

Dr. *JOHNSON*.

Whenever you will, my dear. I am entirely dependent upon my friends.

> [*She takes his hand, kisses it, and goes out, leaving him alone with Mrs. Desmoulins.*

Mrs. *DESMOULINS*.

Would you like a book, sir?

Dr. *JOHNSON*.

No, — yes, a book should help us to enjoy life or endure it. Bring me a small book; a book that can be held readily in the hand is the most useful after all.

Mrs. *DESMOULINS*.

[*Going to the table and fetching several small volumes.*] There is a knock on the door. [*Mrs. Desmoulins goes to the door and opens it.*]

Sir JOSHUA REYNOLDS *enters, goes up to Dr. Johnson, and greets him tenderly.*

Sir *JOSHUA*.

My dear friend, you have, I think, a better colour than when I saw you last. We shall soon have you about again.

Dr. *JOHNSON*.

Dr. *JOHNSON*.

You are, sir, one of the kindest friends I ever had. If I wished to speak evil of you, I would not know how to set about it.

Sir *JOSHUA*.

Did you pass a comfortable night?

Dr. *JOHNSON*.

No, sir. I was sleepless and in pain. I thought for a time that my mind was affected; to test myself I composed Latin verses, they were poor verses and I knew that they were poor; this comforted me, for I knew that I had not lost my critical faculties.

Sir *JOSHUA*.

I have just had a letter from our friend Dr. Taylor.

Dr. *JOHNSON*.

[*His mind wandering a little.*] Dr. Taylor?

Sir *JOSHUA*.

Dr. Taylor of Ashbourne, sir. Your old friend and mine, for whom you have in the past written so many sermons. He wrote to say that he was greatly pleased with the portrait.

Dr. *JOHNSON*.

The portrait?

Sir *JOSHUA*.

Why yes, don't you remember? Your portrait that I painted
for

for him: you are leaning slightly forward, there is a red curtain at the back, you thought it made you look too old.

Dr. *JOHNSON*.

Ah, I remember; I know the room in which it is to hang, the room with the crystal lustres. Dr. Taylor was pleased, was he?

Sir *JOSHUA*.

Yes, he said it was an excellent likeness.

Dr. *JOHNSON*.

The chief excellence of a portrait is the resemblance. I think if you will assist me to the table I will write a letter. [*He is assisted to the table, where for a few moments he writes, pausing now and then for a word. When the letter is finished, he hands it to Sir Joshua.*] Will you be good enough to read it? my mind is not, I fear, entirely clear.

Sir *JOSHUA*.

[*Taking the letter and reading it slowly.*] " My dear Madam: Among the earthly felicities by which Heaven has ameliorated the lot of mortals, none is more likely to enhance personal rectitude or promote domestic bliss than the congenial intercourse of friend and friend. I have recently, madam, passed several weeks in your home, cheered by all that prosperity could supply of comfort, and all that friendship may afford of affection. You will not fail to comprehend that I am deeply sensible

sensible of your benefaction. Suffer not your family to forget, dearest of ladies,

> Your most humble and most obedient servant,
> SAM JOHNSON."

An excellent letter, sir, I am sure the recipient will greatly value it.

Dr. *JOHNSON*.

I must try once more. [*Again writes, and then very slowly reads the letter aloud.*] "Mr. Johnson, who came home last night, sends his respects to dear Doctor Burney and all the dear Burneys, little and great." [*To Mrs. Desmoulins.*] When Frank returns will you ask him to deliver the letter to Dr. Burney? Sir Joshua will be good enough to post the other.

Sir *JOSHUA*.

Certainly.

Dr. *JOHNSON*.

An odd thought strikes me: we shall receive no letters in the grave. Where shall I be buried, think you?

Sir *JOSHUA*.

Doubtless in the Poet's Corner in Westminster Abbey.

Dr. *JOHNSON*.

I hope, sir, I may be thought worthy of that honour.

Sir *JOSHUA*.

I am sure of it, sir.

The

The door opens and Mrs. SIDDONS *enters in the manner of a tragedy queen.*

Mrs. *SIDDONS.*

I was told I might enter; I hope I did not disturb, —

Dr. *JOHNSON.*

[*Trying to rise.*] Why, no, madam; I am glad to be disturbed. [*Looking around and observing that no chair is ready for her.*] You, madam, who so often occasion a want of seats to other people, will the more easily excuse the want of one yourself. I am greatly honoured by this attention.

Mrs. *SIDDONS.*

I have but a moment, sir; I am playing Queen Catharine to-night, but Drury Lane is not far and I could not resist the impulse of paying my respects to one I so greatly esteem.

Dr. *JOHNSON.*

It is a fine part and I wish that I could once more hobble to the theatre myself. Catharine is a noble part.

Mrs. *SIDDONS.*

Sometimes when I play less noble parts, I think of your lines:

> "*The drama's laws, the drama's patrons give,*
> *And we who live to please must please to live.*"

Dr. *JOHNSON.*

It is good of you, madam, to remember them: I am *pénétré* with your kindness.

Mrs. *SIDDONS.*

MRS. SIDDONS

From a Portrait by Gilbert Stuart

Mrs. *SIDDONS*.

My time is up; may I come again?

Dr. *JOHNSON*.

I am, alas, always at home, madam.

[*She shakes his hand, bows, and goes out.*

Enter Frank *with Dr.* Brocklesby, *an old friend, who greets the Doctor tenderly.*

Dr. *BROCKLESBY*.

Sir, as I came through the Strand I met that rake, Jack Wilkes. He inquired very kindly after you and desired me to give you his best respects.

Dr. *JOHNSON*.

That is good of Jack! How many years ago it is that I first met him—at Mr. Dilly's table! He bore an evil reputation in those days.

Dr. *BROCKLESBY*.

And still does, I fear.

Dr. *JOHNSON*.

I hope he does not deserve it. As I grow older I think better of mankind and am prepared to call a man a good man on easier terms than heretofore—not that I would call Jack a good man, but he is a man of parts: he keeps the ball of conversation rolling swiftly. Freedom from pain, and conversation, is all I require to make me happy.

Dr. *BROCKLESBY*.

Dr. *BROCKLESBY.*

I have come to do what I can,—

Dr. *JOHNSON.*

"Can'st thou not minister to a mind diseas'd;
Pluck from the memory a rooted sorrow;
Raze out the written troubles of the brain;
And, with some sweet oblivious antidote,
Cleanse the stuff'd bosom of that perilous stuff
Which weighs upon the heart?"

Dr. *BROCKLESBY.*

"Therein the patient
Must minister to himself."

Dr. *JOHNSON.*

But if he cannot, sir! To die is dreadful.

"To go we know not where;
To lie in cold obstruction and to rot;
This sensible warm motion to become
A kneaded clod—"

*Knock on the door, which is opened by Mrs. Desmoulins, who is in
constant attendance. Enter Mr. WINDHAM and Miss BURNEY.
They greet Dr. Johnson very quietly in turn.*

Dr. *JOHNSON.*

Fanny! dear Burney, you were in my mind when a short time
ago I wrote a note to your father.

Miss *BURNEY.*

Miss *BURNEY*.

I have just heard of your return from Oxford; the journey was, I hope, a pleasant one.

Dr. *JOHNSON*.

Yes, but I was glad to get home. This is not [*looking around*] Streatham, but my friends are about me, all except one.

Miss *BURNEY*.

Do not mention her name, sir, I blush and weep for my sex when I think of her.

Dr. *JOHNSON*.

Have you heard from her?

Miss *BURNEY*.

No, sir, I would not permit her to write to me however much she desired to do so. She is, I hear, with Signor Piozzi in Milan.

Dr. *JOHNSON*.

I hope she may be happy. I owe her a debt of gratitude for unnumbered acts of kindness and of love.

Mr. *WINDHAM*.

I am glad to hear you speaking kindly of her, sir; for wit, genius, generosity, and superlative powers of entertainment, I have not met her equal.

Dr. *JOHNSON*.

Nor have I, sir.

Miss *BURNEY*.

Miss *BURNEY*.

But she was licentious.

Dr. *JOHNSON*.

Why no, Fanny, do not say so. That she should prefer the company of Signor Piozzi to that of a very sick old man is but natural, as it is perhaps but natural that the sick old man should have resented it.

Mr. *WINDHAM*.

Does it not affect you unfavourably, sir, having so many of us in your room? I will withdraw—

Dr. *JOHNSON*.

No, sir, I am glad to have my friends about me. I have always desired to escape from myself. I wish Jamie Boswell were here. [*Sudden attack of coughing seizes the Doctor, who has returned to the large chair.*] Oh, sir, you cannot conceive with what acceleration I advance towards death.

Dr. *BROCKLESBY*.

[*Who comes up to him.*] I fear it is so.

Dr. *JOHNSON*.

I will be conquered. I will not capitulate.

Mr. *WINDHAM*.

Permit me to arrange your pillow. I think I may be able to make you easier. [*Arranges pillow.*]

Dr. *JOHNSON*.

Dr. *JOHNSON*.

That will do—all that a pillow can do. [*Turning towards Dr. Brocklesby.*] Tell me plainly, sir, is it possible for me to recover?

Dr. *BROCKLESBY*.

[*Bowing his head.*] I fear it is not possible.

Dr. *JOHNSON*.

Then, sir, I will take no more physic, not even opiates. I have prayed to God that I might render up my soul to Him unclouded.

Mrs. *DESMOULINS*.

Mr. Burke is coming up the stair.

Dr. *JOHNSON*.

Dear Burke, one of the finest minds in England. He and the Lord Chancellor — they tax all my powers — it is good of him to come.

Enter Mr. EDMUND BURKE.

Mr. *BURKE*.

[*To Mr. Windham, who greets him quietly at the door.*] How is he?

Mr. *WINDHAM*.

This is the end, I think. He is failing fast.

Mr. *BURKE*.

[*Giving his hand to Dr. Johnson.*] I have been detained at the House. I hope you are not uncomfortable.

Dr. *JOHNSON*.

Dr. *JOHNSON*.

My pains have left me, but I am very weak. Dear 'Mund, the end cannot be far, but I have no fear.

Mr. *BURKE*.

Why should you, sir? Your conscience is clear. You have by precept and by example taught us how to live, and we may, from you, learn how to leave this world with Christian resignation.

Dr. *JOHNSON*.

Do some act of kindness every day. [*His mind wanders.*] Put a stone on dear Tetty's grave, a deep, massy stone.

Mrs. *DESMOULINS*.

[*Going up to him.*] I think I detect a change in his breathing.

Dr. *BROCKLESBY*.

[*Taking Dr. Johnson's hand.*] His mind comes and goes fitfully.

Mr. *BURKE*.

For God's sake, sir, can nothing be done? I would go to the end of the earth to save him.

[*It is evident that Dr. Johnson is quite unconscious of what is going on around him. As Mr. Burke passes the table he inadvertently sweeps to the floor a sheet of paper which Mr. Windham picks up.*]

Mr. *WINDHAM*.

What is this? A Prayer to his Maker. [*Reading.*] "Almighty and merciful Father, to Thee be thanks and praise for all
Thy

Thy mercies, for the awakening of my mind, and the op-
portunity now granted of commemorating the death of Thy
Son, Jesus Christ, our Mediator and Redeemer. Enable me,
O Lord, to repent truly of my sins. Enable me by Thy Holy
Spirit to lead hereafter a better life, teach me to form good
resolutions and bring them to effect, and when Thou shalt
finally call me to another state, receive me to everlasting happiness for Our Lord Jesus Christ's sake."

ALL.

[*Very reverently.*] Amen.

Mr. *BURKE.*

Proud and unyielding to those above him in rank, kindly and
considerate to those beneath him in station, humble and pros-
trate before his God. Oh, Samuel Johnson, what a man thou
wert!

Miss *BURNEY.*

I should be going.

Sir *JOSHUA.*

We should remain, I think. He runs a race with death.

Dr. *JOHNSON.*

[*Coming to himself.*] The race is almost run.

Mr. *BURKE.*

I am afraid, sir, such a number of us may be oppressive to
you.

Dr. *JOHNSON.*

Dr. *JOHNSON*.

No, sir, it is not so; and I must be in a wretched state indeed when your company would not be a delight to me.

Mr. *BURKE*.

My dear sir, you have always been too good to me.

Dr. *JOHNSON*.

My friends, remember me in your prayers, and forgive my acts of rudeness. Tetty, dear girl,—

Mr. *BURKE*.

His mind wanders; he is thinking of his wife on whose grave a stone has just been laid.

Sir *JOSHUA*.

What a man he was in his prime! What a towering intellect he had!

> "Take him for all in all,
> I shall not look upon his like again."

Mr. *BURKE*.

Nor any of us. You, sir, have made the Doctor immortal with your brush. I wonder if Boswell will carry out his intention and write his life?

Sir *JOSHUA*.

No doubt of it. He has been collecting material for twenty years and will do it very well. He will write as though he
were

SIR JOSHUA REYNOLDS
From a Drawing after the picture by Himself

were under oath. Johnson's wisdom and his wit must be embalmed for posterity. His talk must be made a matter of record.

Miss BURNEY.

Ah, sir, with all his wisdom and learning he had more comical humour and love of nonsense than anybody I ever saw.

Mr. WINDHAM.

And no man could turn a compliment more neatly than he: while he was a scholar, he was also a man of the world. I once heard him say: "I live in the world and I take in some degree the colour of the world as it moves along."

The passage door opens and a YOUNG GIRL *enters.*

YOUNG GIRL.

Oh, gentlemen, I must see him. I never met him, but he is so good. He sent word to me that he would see me if he were dying. Only for a moment, sir.

Mr. WINDHAM.

Only for a moment. You may be too late.

Dr. JOHNSON.

[*Rousing himself.*] I am glad you have come: come close to me. [*She kneels beside his chair and takes his hand. There is complete silence.*]

YOUNG GIRL.

You said I might come to you, if you were dying.

Dr. JOHNSON.

Dr. *JOHNSON.*

I am dying. [*Raising his hands over her head.*] God bless you, my dear. [*He dies.*]

Dr. *BROCKLESBY.*

He is beyond the aid of man.

Sir *JOSHUA.*

[*In tears.*] My dear, dear friend! His death will make a chasm which nothing can fill.

Mr. *WINDHAM.*

Boswell should give his biography an epic character. What life save his would bear such critical inspection?

Mr. *BURKE.*

None. It is well with a man when he comes to die to have nothing heavier upon his conscience than having been a little rough in conversation.

CURTAIN.